The Entrepreneurial Standard

Taking Your Company from Garage to Great

By
Tanya McCaffery

Published by Efluential Publishing

To my husband, Ed, who has loved me through everything, supports me in all my adventures and who has told me I'm crazy, but that it's a good thing.

To my parents, who gave me the entrepreneurial spirit which included my mom teaching me that accounting didn't have to be complicated to be effective.

And to my three boys, who are the reason for everything I do.

I love you all.

TABLE OF CONTENTS

INTRODUCTION

David and Goliath

Never in the history of our economy has there been more of a disparity between big business and small.

It's a typical David and Goliath saga. Small business contributes so much to our overall economy and business infrastructure. So, why aren't big businesses listening? Wake up, economy. David won! The underdog is the hero in our and every other economy in the history of commercial enterprise. Small businesses are cited as playing a leading role in our current economic resurgence. While David's intentions were less commercial in nature than a classic entrepreneur's passion, the story line remains the same. The underdog can be ruled out, bet against....considered all but defeated. At that moment where they are seemingly out of contention, the underdog can do amazing things. The entrepreneur can start something where there previously was nothing. Entrepreneurs create their own value proposition – whether their product serves an unanswered niche, satisfies an urgency in the marketplace or helps solve an unavoidable problem.

Small business – David – needs a strong positive trajectory, financial security for the original stakeholders, access to lending and more internal bandwidth.

Big business continues at the same pace. You can find big businesses out there that are more innovative than others that are described as entrepreneurial in nature. But at the same time, there are established systems, routines and culture in a big business. The executive team can revise and improve existing norms in a big business when the time is right, but for the most part big business does not have to re-create their own wheel. Their foundation has been built by their predecessors. Big business – Goliath – needs shareholder approval, revenues of a massive scale, thousands of employees, and legal departments. Goliath holds out his hand for government bailout and protection via regulation.

The nimble and hungrier David can outpace and ultimately defeat the unsuspecting and over-confident Goliath with fervor and passion that run the gamut from unbridled innovation to a no-rules attitude to a kill-or-be-killed resolution. There is more at stake than shareholder approval in a small business. Entrepreneurs don't just move on to the next job if their venture fails like a banker passed from bank to bank in the wake of a collapse as if nothing ever happened. They have much more skin in the game.

What would happen if David took the best of both worlds and combined them to his advantage? If he kept his nimble, agile, starved passion and paired it with the structure, leverage and systems of big business. That is how you build a better bicycle. By taking the strengths of David and the strengths of Goliath and combining them into one uber-competitive, innovative, yet structured weapon of mass commercialization, you would have an entity that is set to excel and that has all of the tools from both big and small to dominate their marketplace.

Economic Personalities

There is a standoff in how large businesses and small businesses interact. Of course, they need each other to survive in a perfect economic eco-system – peddling each other's wares as they go about their business. But, every single entrepreneur you talk to has their own story about a big business that did them wrong – a bank that called a loan, a merchant processing company that held their receipts, a vendor that racked up their pricing, a supplier that didn't deliver. That experience can leave a small business helpless and infuriated. The small business has had to scramble and deploy considerable internal resources to mitigate the damage while the big business unsympathetically cites underwriting criteria, checkboxes, and standard protocol.

The sheer volume of buying power that the small business community possesses is a major factor in our overall domestic and global economy. But, because the fury of small business passion is millions upon millions of small voices rather than one large resounding voice, that power becomes diluted to the point that a single small business fighting against the oppression of a large corporation can make that small business appear to be more of a speck that can be flicked off the corporate shoulder of the conglomerate.

This is why there are organizations and lobbying groups, often within a single field, designed to amass a large number of those small business voices and create one larger voice with a common interest. It is also why entrepreneurs need to work smarter to stay one step ahead of not only their competition but also the large businesses that they need for their company to operate.

Our modern market culture is permeated with two major personalities. The personality of big business is perceived as oppressive and unresponsive. In recent years, the previously benign term "Wall Street" drips with animosity and disdain. It is a descriptor in and of itself. It beckons images of corporate abuse and widespread malfeasance. It also conjures in the entrepreneur's mind the post-traumatic stress of a big business that has previously wronged them with unreasonable demands.

On the flip side, the entrepreneurial personality has come to be complimentary. It also acts as a synonym of "innovative". To say that someone possesses entrepreneurial spirit creates an image of hope, passion and tenacity. Even describing a huge corporation as "entrepreneurial" paints them in a better light. What are some large corporations that you would describe as entrepreneurial? I'm sure you could quickly rattle off several – Apple, Zappos and Google to name a few.

Small businesses operate differently than a big business. Small businesses have the luxury and power to be nimble, to react quickly and to turn on a dime. Large corporations can be sluggish and unresponsive to immediate stimuli – like turning a freightliner. They are often resolute in their processes and while many large corporations possess the innovative spirit to some degree they are also much more proceduralized and documented in their processes.

There are advantages and disadvantages to both modes of action. Being able to move quickly allows small businesses to take advantage of opportunities as they present themselves and it also allows them to react quickly and mitigate a negative situation. Large corporations can often be the butt of jokes referencing their rigid and unyielding nature, but many facets of large businesses could benefit entrepreneurial companies by helping them grow and meet their goals.

The Entrepreneurial Standard at Work

To entrepreneurs, it's a brand new day each and every day. It's passion, devotion and giving up all for the greater good of the company. Entrepreneurs often sacrifice themselves and sometimes their very own financial stability to risk it all in the venture. It's innovation and it's truly genuine customer service.

But small businesses are held back by more limited resources – no huge ad campaigns, smaller technology budgets, less funds overall. The passionate underdog. Small businesses are much more likely to bootstrap their operation, run with less than documented procedures and have inconsistent quality in their products and in their customer service.

Small businesses can create their own limiting ceiling by not putting in place things that big businesses – or businesses that became big – figured out were necessary if they were to sustain massive amounts of growth. Many small businesses can limit their success by making it dependent upon the individual bandwidth of the founder or entrepreneur – which is finite. But, the collective capacity of all resources that can be enlisted by your company to aid its growth is unlimited. If you employ these infinite resources to increase your company's bandwidth, then you will instill sustainable, profitable upward momentum.

Here we will look at cases of small business persecution by big businesses, and how entrepreneurs can turn the tables to use these antics to their advantage. We will delve into details and actionable steps to show how some big business practices can help small businesses be stronger. There are massive amounts of stories of small businesses becoming huge successes throughout history. We will analyze the small business contribution to our economy and also dig into case studies of companies that have become huge corporations from meager beginnings.

As a small business trying to grow and excel, how do you take the snippets of really great ideas from big corporations and put them to work for you within your company?

By putting in place things like institutional level controls, reporting, processes and structure, while staying true to your firm's core beliefs, your business can also have the bandwidth, systems and discipline to reach the highest benchmarks you have set for it and for yourself.

This is the Entrepreneurial Standard.

Chapter One

AN ECONOMY IN CRISIS

The Playground

Imagine this. You are standing in the middle of your third grade playground. It is a warm, spring day. Summer break is getting ever closer and you have big plans for this beautiful weather. You think about the forts you will build, adventures you will embark on, treasures you will discover. You are alive in the moment of this spring day full of opportunity and adventure. You are entrepreneurship.

Before you can breathe in another deep breath of the fresh spring air, you are approached by the playground bully. He is in the process of stealing lunch money from the kids on the playground. You see that you are his next target. Your chest tightens, and you abandon thoughts of adventure and freedom. The sky doesn't seem quite so bright or so blue.

The slovenly, slow, insecure bully makes his way around the playground striking fear into the kids he encounters. He has no real talents to speak of. He operates from a position of fear, terrorism and volume with no sincere empathy for any of his victims.

It's a negative palpable energy, isn't it? You can feel this bully approaching as if you were once again that child standing exposed on the playground in third grade. This is the large corporation.

Corporate Terrorists

Big business acts like the playground bully. Many of them are taking the lunch money of the entire economy. They are corporate terrorists.

Corporate terrorists come in many shapes and forms. While an interaction with an inflexible big business can leave you blaming that entire corporation for your plight, the truth is that it all starts with an individual interaction.

There is a phenomenon in many large corporations that I call corporate-think. There is a high level or middle manager somewhere, maybe they have been given a little more power lately, and they need to flex their corporate muscles. They will say "no." They will give reasons such as that is not per our standard operating procedure. It is not in the budget. That is not allowed by our protocols. This is not in line with our risk tolerance standards.

These are the biggest offenders in the corporate terrorist realm. They come with nameless, faceless titles like underwriter, risk manager, customer service manager, vice president of corporate compliance. They are the antithesis to the entrepreneurial way of doing things. They are completely removed from the way things are done in small businesses much less do they have any interest in letting small businesses get things done.

Unfortunately, these managers can wreak havoc on an entrepreneur's operation because small business needs big business in order to offer its services. Whether it's a small business that uses a large bank for its banking, borrowing or transaction processing or one that uses a large vendor to provide the materials the small business sells, big business can go for the jugular if they see something in the small business that doesn't work within their rules or fit in their box.

In order for a small business to not only survive, but also thrive they must develop ways to insulate themselves from the effect that corporate terrorists have on their operation.

Too Big to Fail

Some big businesses have been deemed "too big to fail" as if all of the other businesses and consumers are junkies with no real options, pining away for the drugs they peddle into the commercial marketplace.

"Too big to fail" basically means that in a free economy if a large corporation were to fail, the fallout, and the way that failure would affect each and every one of us, would be much worse than the cost of bailing them out and aiding them to stand on their own two feet – like an ailing geriatric patient that can't be expected to be strong or to even know any better.

The term has been used more frequently in recent years as it was determined that certain financial institutions were so deeply woven into economic systems that their failure would be disastrous to the economy. Critics of the concept believed that recipients of the aid were more motivated to act immorally and actually profit from the bailouts they received. This was why there was so much focus in those years on capping compensation and perks to executives and the boards of companies receiving Federal assistance.

Past Federal Reserve President Alan Greenspan was a vocal critic of the policy, saying, "If they're too big to fail, then they're too big." The necessity for aid and the possibility of failure was believed by opponents to be the result of the organization's inability to properly manage risk and that they should be left to fail regardless of the consequences.

In his book *Financing Failure*, Vern McKinley examines the policy decisions that led to the recent bailouts and compares them to attempted government interventions dating as far back as the 1930s. He delivers a clear and expertly researched analysis of how the bailouts emerged from a rationale of necessity and fear and that they were deliberately designed to prevent the public from reviewing the decision-making process, ultimately at tremendous cost to taxpayers.

From 1985 to 1999, McKinley worked with the Board of Governors of the Federal Reserve, the Federal Deposit Insurance Corporation (FDIC), the Resolution Trust Corporation and the Treasury's Office of Thrift Supervision. Since 1999, he has applied this expertise as a legal advisor to a laundry list of governments on their financial policies. Countries like China, Nigeria, Ukraine, Kazakhstan, Vietnam, Latvia, Morocco, Afghanistan and many more look to McKinley for his expertise in financial and regulatory policy especially in the face of a financial crisis.

McKinley has been a vocal skeptic of the bailouts and other financial debacles in recent times and has been steadfast in his stance on the history of financial crises over the past century stating that this situation is something we have seen over and over again in history. McKinley sees a common cycle occur in these situations. A big bank gets close to failure, the regulators go into denial, they figure out there's a problem and then they panic and tell woeful stories of how bad it will be – a la Chicken Little – if they don't do something to stop it. Terms like "contagion" and "systemic risk" send the public into a tailspin and make the aid to the ailing banks a reality. As an important byproduct to McKinley's work in this area, the public now has a greater awareness of trends of financial crisis and bailouts in history and therefore can be more informed of the true threat, or lack thereof, that a failure poses to their economic reality.

While the term "too big to fail" has predominantly been used with respect to financial institutions, other notable bailouts have occurred recently that have questionable levels of success. The auto industry bailout in 2008 assisted three major US automakers to the tune of $80 billion. Chrysler and General Motors held out their hands for relief. Ford was named as one of the automakers that were to receive assistance but their CEO at first declared they didn't need it. Ultimately, they didn't receive the same assistance as GM and Chrysler but instead received government loans through a program of the DOE. I can't blame Ford for wanting to stay on a level playing field.

The auto industry contributes a material amount of output and jobs to the US economy. At the time of the bailout, the auto industry contributed $500 billion to the total US GDP output. A 30% decline in auto sales would translate directly to a 1% decrease in overall economic output. As sales and number of jobs plummeted, the idea that they were too big to fail became more evident and the bailout came to be. Ironically, at the time, many analysts felt that Chrysler would fail with or without the bailout and Ford didn't really need it, so the primary focus of the bailout became saving jobs at General Motors.

Ultimately, the US government shelled out $80 billion toward the bailout of the auto industry. As of the fall of 2013, it had recovered $54.6 billion of that money with the rest being held in various types of securities.

In the end was the bailout a success? A detailed discussion of that point is fodder for many books, reports and essays on that subject alone. But, for our purposes here, the answer is…it depends.

It depends on who you ask and also on how you gauge success. In late 2013, the Treasury Department announced that it lost over $10 billion when it closed out its position in General Motors. While Chrysler paid back its loans, the US Government reported that it ultimately lost $1.9 billion on the Chrysler bailout. One can find volumes of additional reports on the bailouts that define it as the fallout of mismanagement and non-competitive labor rates rather than lack of demand for the core product lines. Definitely not a success in my book.

At the same time, the Center for Automotive Research released a report on the bailout and in that report stated that it saved hundreds of thousands of US jobs and that the combined tax revenues to the US government from these jobs contributed far more than the bailout itself cost including any losses incurred. Sounds more like a success.

Nonetheless, the point here is the bailouts demonstrated overall that a business that is big enough can obtain an irrational amount of support regardless of how they manage their companies or finances. Not so true in the small business sector.

The Vulnerability of Entrepreneurs

What do you think small businesses would do with that volume of subsidy? Ironically, a large part of the bailout and TARP – the Troubled Asset Relief Plan – was geared toward mitigating the financial crisis for all business and not just big business. Yet the effect on small business seems all but lost.

The SBA Office of Advocacy sponsored a report issued in 2012 and written by Rebel Cole of DePaul University. It was called "How Did the Financial Crisis Affect Small Business Lending in the United States?" No small business owner needs a government-issued report to tell them that the effect was abysmal. In fact, the report's introduction starts with the seemingly innocent statement "Anecdotal evidence suggested that small businesses, which largely rely upon banks for credit, were especially hard hit." Brilliant. Yes, that much we know.

Small business lending in the period from 2008 through 2010 definitely dried up and as a small business, it was almost impossible to secure any type of additional financing from traditional lenders. The report goes on to provide data on just how much the small business sector was hit by lack of funds.

In 1994, bank lending to small business was at $308 billion and rose to a peak of $659 billion in June of 2008. It then plummeted to a balance of only $543 billion in 2011 – a drop of almost 18%. Bank lending to all firms (which includes small and big business) was at $758 billion in 1994 and rose to a peak of $2.14 trillion in June 2008. It then dropped to $1.96 trillion in 2011 – a decrease of less than 9%. This shows that small business access to funds dropped by twice that of the economy overall.

Even more insulting is that if you remove the totals of small business lending from the overall lending totals, it shows that lending to big business only decreased by 4% during the same time frame that small business lending dropped by 18%! This is aside from all of the bailout and subsidy funds that big businesses received in the same time frame. Small businesses were left to fend for themselves and get creative on finding sources of liquidity to fund their operations.

With TARP, almost $200 billion in capital was injected into banks in the hopes of spurring lending – especially to small business. In the SBA Office of Advocacy report, an interesting finding is that in line with the decrease in overall lending detailed above, banks that received TARP funds decreased their lending to small businesses by even more than banks that did not receive TARP funds.

What made matters worse and what isn't immediately apparent in the totals above were the egregious amounts of debt that were called by the banks. When a bank calls a note, they are basically saying, "Thanks for playing, but something about you or your loan made us nervous and we need you to give it back. Now." Small businesses were facing huge paybacks of debt while being unable to get more.

Now, to be fair, in the Economic Stimulus Package, there was a big focus on providing economic stimulus to small businesses in the form of tax credits that were estimated to be $54 billion. But the tax credits revolved around spending money. They were focused on hiring veterans, writing off machinery and equipment, and giving bigger raises. None of which was relevant to a company, strapped for cash, unable to get financing whose owners were missing paycheck after paycheck and thus not spending any money.

There was another subset of cuts designed to increase the guarantees on SBA loans and eliminate fees for certain SBA loan programs. Bob Hope once said "A bank is a place that will lend you money if you can prove that you don't need it." Small businesses desperately needed it. So, again, the stimulus was not relevant to struggling small businesses unable to make it past the underwriter's icy glare and get approved.

The SBA applauded the Obama administration for this contribution to the small business community in 2009. This was before their studies on the state of small business were released in 2012 that paint a somewhat different picture of how it all played out.

We don't know for sure the exact toll that the recent recession took on the overall small business community. We do know that according to the US Census Bureau rather than the norm of increasing numbers of small businesses each year, there were a little more than 337,000 fewer small businesses in 2011 than there were before the recession – and chances are that lack of available funding was a contributor.

Rather than contract the funding given to small businesses and exponentially expand the lending, subsidies and bailouts given to large corporations that could not provide for themselves, imagine for a moment those funds in the hands of a virile community of entrepreneurs.

I tend to believe that an economy where the real volumes of resources are placed in the hands of the true innovators would be an economy destined for success. The passionate entrepreneurs would create the products and services to fill the niches that create a strong economy rather than the current model that continues to pump regular gasoline into a premium unleaded world.

Chapter Two

SMALL BUSINESS CONTRIBUTIONS EQUAL HUGE GAINS FOR US ALL

A Force to Be Reckoned With

Small business plays a vital role in the economy of the United States. Small businesses are incubators for innovation and employment growth anytime – but especially during times of economic recovery.

The Small Business Administration defines a small business as one having fewer than 500 employees. According to Forbes, over 50% of the working population in the United States works in a small business. In 2010, the Census Bureau estimated that there were 28 million small businesses in the United States – and that number keeps growing. They make up over 99% of the employer firms in the country and are responsible for 46% of private sector output. They comprise 98% of firms exporting to other countries and 33% of the value of all exports. Small businesses are also busy at work creating almost two-thirds of new private sector jobs – which is broken down 60/40 between growth in existing establishments versus startups that are popping up everywhere.

US gross domestic product or GDP is the market value of the goods and services produced by labor and property in the United States. It is the job of the Small Business Administration to conduct studies periodically that measure the contribution to GDP of small versus large business. The most recent was written by Kathryn Kobe of Economic Consulting Services, LLC, and sponsored by the SBA Office of Advocacy in 2012. It covered the period ending with 2010.

According to the study, small business has in recent years contributed a material portion of the total US GDP. In 1998, the study reflected that small business contributed 50.5% – more than half – of US GDP. This number increased to 50.7 % by 2004, but then dropped to 46% in 2008, proving that small businesses were especially hard hit by the recession. Data from the SBA study through 2010 showed that while both large and small businesses were affected, small businesses had a harder time recovering than large corporations and thus were affected longer.

In 2010, the SBA sponsored a separate study written by Major L. Clark and Radian Saade entitled "The Role of Small Business in Economic Development of the United States: From the End of the Korean War (1953) to

Present." In the study, Clark and Saade contend that small business is an engine of economic growth and job creation and that not tapping into the strength of small business delays rather than promotes growth. They go on to argue that if the US is to continue to grow, small business must be a major part in order to lead the US economy to the next level. Otherwise the "past is prologue."

The overall study analyzes various platforms of legislation over the past half century that were aimed to stimulate the economy such as the Labor Surplus Program, the 1977 Local Public Works Act, the HUBZone Act, the Stafford Act and concluding with the American Recovery and Reinvestment Act of 2009.

They ultimately conclude that "these tools and actions failed to incorporate comprehensively the unique and valuable perspective of the nation's economic strength – the small business community." This is obviously an enormous missed opportunity in our economy's recovery and growth.

The unappreciative trend toward small business contribution has a long running history. In 1944 in his State of the Union address, President Franklin D. Roosevelt presented his infamous economic bill of rights. This bill of rights outlined a plan to ensure a productive and well paid job to all Americans – he called it "useful and remunerative" – which would in turn create a secure economy. The president's cabinet referred often to "full productivity" and "full employment". Noticeably lacking in the "New Deal" planning was any reference whatsoever to the role that small business would play in the continued recovery after the Great Depression. The focal point was national recovery with no real emphasis on small business. For many years, this notion seemed to be political lip service. If it had focused more on the contribution of entrepreneurs and startups, maybe the theories would have met with more success.

The Move to Local

In more recent times, small business continues to gain momentum and visibility. There isn't a consumer anywhere that hasn't become vested in or at least keenly aware of the local movement. Small business has launched into the stratosphere in terms of global awareness. The small business has become an icon for producing products that are sustainable, ethical and humane while at the same time injecting funds back into their local economies in the form of sales taxes, wages paid to employees, and much more.

Large corporations have joined the movement in also touting their products to meet the same criteria but the premise of the movement remains small business. "Buy Local, Think Global" now makes it sound like shopping at small businesses makes you a better person. Without getting into the environmental and social reasons for this, from a consumer perspective, it does. With the contribution that small business makes to the economy and their ability to think and act quickly, chances are that the dollar you spend at the small business will be more effective in promoting economic growth overall than a dollar spent at a large box store.

American Express figured out the contribution of small business and began the campaign "Small Business Saturday" to promote shopping at small businesses in a big way. The mantras of the campaign say things like "Small Businesses Are the Heartbeats of our Communities" and "Every Neighborhood Needs a Champion." Small businesses can pay ad dollars toward being included in the collateral for the day of shopping designated as Small Business Saturday. This particular Saturday falls right after Black Friday, when consumers get up any time after midnight on Thanksgiving night to hit holiday sales at most of the large shopping chains.

Small Business Saturday is a serendipitous partnership. While most, if not all, small businesses cannot pay to run a TV ad in the middle of a football game on Thanksgiving Day, American Express can. Small businesses get the additional traffic that a company like American Express can market and American Express gets the additional processing fees from small businesses that do well on Small Business Saturday. American Express can be genuinely applauded for recognizing the power of the small business economic contribution.

The Entrepreneur as a Consumer

Small businesses not only produce large portions of the US GDP, large businesses target small businesses as customers. The purchasing power of small business is growing exponentially. Just watch any FedEx, Intuit, Office Depot or Microsoft ad. The people in those commercials are primarily small businesses.

Think about the last commercial you saw with the slogan "What can Brown do for you?" This was an entire sixty seconds based on how UPS streamlined the shipping and logistics for a small company and freed up the time of the owner. UPS does not run ads on how they can free up the time of the CEO of a large corporation, because it has become commonplace that the CEO of a large corporation wouldn't be caught dead in the shipping department. Fortune 500 CEOs don't lick their own stamps. Entrepreneurs often do. Therefore, it is usually the owner of the small business making decisions on how to spend the money of a small company and that spending adds up.

PEX Card, a company that provides prepaid expense cards for businesses, began conducting annual benchmark expense surveys in 2012 and issued their second annual report in March 2014. The survey covers a variety of topics related to how small and medium businesses spend their money.

The very first question asked in the survey in 2013 was "If you could identify one thing that keeps you up at night, what is it?" The top answer at 22% was expenses eating into profits, and the survey goes on to show that small businesses are spending some serious dough. The group of survey responders reported anywhere from $363,000 to $2.3 million in expenses per company per year in the survey categories which covered everything from rent to marketing. It also showed that across the board expenses of small businesses were higher in 2013 than 2012 – as much as 51.8% higher, fueled by a combination of growth and greater numbers of companies.

Small businesses are a force to be reckoned with and make up the lion's share of the purchases of business-related products. Standing together, small businesses are a demographic that would devastate a large corporation if they took their business elsewhere.

It's Always a Great Time to Be an Entrepreneur

Small businesses can become more notable and numerous in periods of economic decline even without staunch political support – or maybe to spite the lack of support. Contrary to what your instinct may be telling you, starting a business during challenging economic times has historically proved to be a good prospect.

Within every adversity lies the seed of an equal or greater opportunity. While the government passes new legislation to spur economic growth, much of it ill-suited to meet the challenges that small businesses face, entrepreneurs press on.

In fact, it seems that companies started during trying economic times have better survival skills in general. In a recession, many frustrated job hunters throw up their hands and say, "Maybe I'll just start a business!" Which just might be a great idea! Good ideas and great products are always in demand. Especially successful in times of decline are companies that solve a pressing problem.

By starting a company with a product that serves a need, that entrepreneur is creating their own wealth and also creating economic output to spur the overall economy. Being an entrepreneur can come with a sense of control – control of your schedule, control of your income, control of decisions. This is liberating in good times and bad.

Tough times have spawned the next generation of great companies. Over half of the Dow 30 were started during recessions. GE started during the economic panic of 1873, Disney started in the economic recession of the 1920s, HP began during the Great Depression and Microsoft started during the recession of 1975.

Be Prepared for the Hard Work and Tough Decisions

Don't take any of this to mean that starting a small business in the midst of an economic meltdown is a walk in the park. Starting and running a successful small business in any economy is one of the most difficult jobs out there. You have to really want it and you have to be willing to give up a lot to make it work.

As Ella Brennan of the infamous New Orleans brunch spot Brennan's puts it regarding the Great Depression and the small business spirit: "I mean it was a terrible time, but I think it's like most things in life. It has a lot to do with attitude. You can bitch, and gripe, and complain all you want. Or you can make do." And she and her family made do. They were self-reliant, enterprising, and made every dollar stretch farther and now several generations later, the restaurant is still a huge success and relies on many lessons taught it by the Great Depression.

There are many companies that lose – or almost lose – their businesses during hard times that learn to run them better. Sometimes scaling back is what it takes. Bigger is not always better. Bigger can mean more overhead, more employees and more liability. "Pursue your passion. Business is tougher than ever during a recession. You have to fight for orders and overcome challenges. If you're passionate, you're contagious. People want to work with you, buy from you, work for you, and invest in you," says Rich Sloan, founder of Startup Nation.

No matter your passion, don't forget about profitability. Net income must correlate to gross revenues with growth and bottom lines should not shrink as top lines grow. Economic downturns cannot be used as an excuse for negative trends in a small business unless they are very temporary or that small business will not survive.

If a company has $2 million in sales and its owner takes home $500,000, but then the next year has $4 million in sales and its owner only takes home $300,000, that company needs to take a serious look at its financials. Per Eric Siegel, instructor at the University of Pennsylvania's Wharton School of Entrepreneurship "Building revenue is art, cutting expenses is mechanics." Unless the reduction can be explained as part of the company's business plan or reinvestment into the company's growth, this is not a recession proof company. Entrepreneurs must be constantly reviewing the numbers and making the hard decisions quickly when they see unexplainable downward trends.

More at Stake for Entrepreneurs

FDR's New Deal speech included the proclamation that "happiness lies not in the mere possession of money, it lies in the joy of achievement, in the thrill of creative effort, the joy of the moral stimulation of worth. Let me assert my belief that the only thing we have to fear, is fear itself." A Franklin D. Roosevelt fireside chat may or may not say it – but this ideal practically screams "entrepreneur"!

For entrepreneurs, the promise of a future of achievement, contribution and financial security is wonderful. It's what they believe, what keeps them keenly focused on pitfalls in their company's path and what drives their passion in their business every day. But it also drives the fear in an entrepreneur that can contribute to their demise. One of the continuing pervasive trends inhibiting small business recovery and growth post-recession is uncertainty.

Small businesses are far more affected by fear and uncertainty than big business. In small business the stakes are higher. When an entrepreneur loses their job that means their company has failed. This most likely comes with a complete docket of personal financial crisis, fear and instability.

When a large business has financial difficulty, those that are terminated, whether C-level executives or employee level staff, move on to the next gig. Their enemy is unemployment. Sure a past entrepreneur can get a job once their business fails, but chances are they mortgaged their house and invested substantial personal assets to try to make their venture work. Now, as a result, they are very much behind the pack on restructuring their family's financial future. And this doesn't even bring in to the equation the emotional toll that a small business failure can take on an individual and their family – just ask any grandparent that is still talking about the Great Depression and how it affected them. Financial adversity can be very hard to overcome psychologically.

In more recent times, small businesses have seen more than their share of abuse. Whether it was tightening lending policies from banks under TARP, all but fatal healthcare reform with Obamacare, or pressure from mounting tax burdens, entrepreneurs had scarcely a chance to catch their breath after the Great Recession started to subside. But in harmony with the economic spirit, despite lack of financial or regulatory backing, small business remains a force in our global economy. How do they do it?

Chapter Three

FROM GARAGE TO GREAT

Humble Beginnings

How does a company navigate legislative, regulatory and financial pitfalls while surging forward in creating a prosperous company? And once they have a foothold there, how do they then go from being a dream in a garage to being a multi-national corporation with the systems and processes to be able to handle millions of dollars of transactions each month – or even day?

All businesses have to start from the beginning. Some of those beginnings are more humble than others. After all, Coca-Cola started from a copper pot, a note jotted on a piece of paper and $500. Amazon, Apple, Disney, Harley-Davidson and Hewlett-Packard all started in a garage. And we are all familiar with many other success stories of small mom-and-pops that have become gigantic corporations.

McDonald's started from a single hamburger stand purchased from Dick and Mac McDonald by Ray Kroc. Ray Kroc was just like any other entrepreneur pitching his vision to others. His vision was to open McDonald's restaurants all over the US and back when that was just a vision and not history, it met with much doubt and some raised eyebrows. By 1958, McDonald's had sold its 100 millionth hamburger. Today, McDonald's refers to itself as the most successful small business in the world.

Walmart was founded by Sam Walton in 1945 when he purchased, among other locations, a chain of Ben Franklin Stores from the Butler Brothers. Sam Walton started as a small town retailer in the Ozark Mountains of Arkansas. His vision was to sell products at a lower price with a lower profit margin but to offset that by higher volume. The meager beginnings of Walmart saw a cash strapped Sam Walton expanding from location to location sometimes by borrowing money from his father-in-law and often leaving a location because of difficulty negotiating leases with the landlords that saw a retail opportunity in what Sam had done in their property. Sam and his brother Bud logged thousands of hours as pilots in their small plane scouting new locations.

Ford Motor Company was started in 1903 by Henry Ford with $28,000 from investors and the beginning of his vision of the assembly line model. In Henry Ford's time, the automobile was a plaything for the rich. Not the best value proposition. Henry Ford did not invent the car itself, but he produced an automobile that the average American could afford. He did this through his unique method of manufacturing and in the first year alone sold over ten thousand Model T's at a purchase price of $825 each – that is more than $225 million in today's dollars.

While there are many rags to riches stories of companies that made it big over longer periods of tenacious resolve, there is a new phenomenon that occurs when a company comes from small beginnings and becomes a huge conglomerate in the blink of an eye. In today's economy, there are high school students to hip hop stars turned into billionaires overnight when their app or company is acquired. For example, Apple has snatched up everything from Siri to Beats. Google has been a force in this sector – investing over $250 million in Uber, acquiring YouTube, and much more. Google has been acquiring, on average, one company per week since 2010.

Then there's the initial public offering, or IPO. Granted, there are the huge IPOs that on their day of issue grow by thousands of percentage points fueled by things like dot com or credit bubbles. But there are others that top the charts with exponential growth that show more fundamental opportunity. When Whole Foods went public, their market cap increased 1,000% in 25 short quarters. Starbucks did it in 12 quarters. eBay? In just two.

The original Whole Foods opened in 1980 with a staff of only 19 people. You can actually still visit the first

Starbucks near Pike Place Market in Seattle. eBay was started by 25-year-old Pierre Omidyar, who wrote the code for the auction website and as its very first listing sold a broken laser pointer for $14.83. We know now, in retrospect, that these companies are huge. We know their success stories because we see them in the newspaper, discuss them with our peers and co-workers and maybe studied their roads to success case studies in college.

These are companies that started in garages and from meager beginnings. They were one of the underdogs. What changed and what stayed the same? And what are they doing to not just accomplish, but more importantly sustain growth while also sustaining profitability?

The Principles Behind the Entrepreneurial Standard

There are practices in place in large corporations that small businesses can learn from and use to fuel their businesses. They were put in place early on in the companies that met with substantial success and they are at the core of the remaining chapters of this book. Whether it is putting in place institutional-level financial reporting, systematizing your operations to achieve consistent customer experiences or balancing innovation with day-to-day operation, we will go through the large corporation practices you need in your small business in order to grow to whatever level it is you want to see in your future.

Before that, there are fundamental concepts that will also help you get there – paradigms to keep at the core of your growth to ensure you stay the company you want to be while you grow into the company you want to become. Some general guidelines, if you will. Let's go through those first.

1. Build Your Elastic Foundation

Act today like the company you want to become. If you want to become a 100-million-dollar company, refer to yourself today as a 100-million-dollar company. This will ensure that you act with the end in mind.

The path from garage to great can be a very long road. Sometimes it feels like you are in a tuck skiing straight down the mountain with no one in your way. At other times, it can feel like chopping your way with a machete through an overgrown jungle.

In dealing with hundreds of companies in my career, some that stayed small or eventually went away and some that became huge and met all of their benchmarks and goals and everything in between, there is one common theme that has become apparent. The companies that became huge had structure. The ones that stayed small did not. Structure in customer service, product development, finances, and more. Structure that defined who they were, how they did things and how they measured results – and structure that was put in place with the steadfast intent of taking that company to where they ultimately wanted to be. Call it proceduralizing, institutionalizing, Gerberizing or whatever you like, if structure is not defined and policies not implemented, the limitations on the bandwidth of the small business CEO will drive that entrepreneur to extinction.

When putting in place your company's foundation as you start out, build structure that can expand. This will ensure that as your company starts to grow rather than throwing out the model and starting again, you can add to the existing model to accommodate a larger operation. This will save time, resources and energy – three things that no entrepreneur can afford to waste.

2. Answer the Question – Where Is "There"?

The first step is to define what you mean by "great" in your company. I use this as a metaphor for "there". Do you know where your "there" is and do you know what it will look like when you get it?

Defining your goals in specific terms is not just a luxury for the dreamers. Goals are much more attainable if they are stated and quantifiable. If you don't know what your ultimate goal is for your company, not only will you not know when you get there but your chances of getting there in the first place are drastically reduced.

The second step after you define where your "there" is would be to make sure that's what you want. As a company gets larger, your job is not going to get easier. In an interview with David Bradley of *The Atlantic* at the Aspen Institute in summer 2014, Pepsico CEO Indra Nooyi said very candidly, "Women can't have it all."

Indra was appointed CEO of Pepsico in 2006 and is considered currently to be the thirteenth most powerful woman in the world. She is a mother of two and is very vocal about the challenges of balancing work and family life. On the evening of her promotion she arrived at her home around 10'o clock at night only to be greeted by her mother on the stairs from the garage. Her traditional mother sent her to the store for milk and told her no matter her accomplishments at work to remember her role when she's home. As CEO of a Fortune 500 level company and a mother, the demands on Indra's time are immense. Regardless of whether you are male or female, have kids or don't have kids, you need to examine how you see your role in your company evolving as it grows.

There are two categories of companies to consider when making the decision of what you want your company to do for you – growth companies (also referred to as liquidity companies) and lifestyle companies. Where do you see your company on this spectrum? If you see yourself as a growth company, as that growth comes to fruition, the demands it places on your time will increase. You will need to make tough decisions that involve longer hours, more boards, possibly additional travel and much more. On the flipside, a lifestyle company's focus is on sustainable income but with more time for you. You will still be in the driver's seat of being an entrepreneur with all of the advantages and disadvantages of being self-employed, but there is a solid focus on work/life balance. The company's primary role becomes providing you the lifestyle you would like, whether that means financially or having more time with your children.

Go through the process of determining what your ultimate goal is for your company and for yourself. Make it as detailed as possible and put in place executable steps to ensure progress as well as benchmarks to measure success. After all, it's much easier to get where you are going if you have a map.

3. Focus on Your Company's Sureties

Isaac Newton said, "If you can learn to stand on the shoulders of giants, you will get bigger faster." Whether it's giants you rely on or products that allow you to specialize in what you're good at and not dilute your resources by recreating the wheel, you will grow faster by doing just what you do best while taking some lessons from those trailblazers that have found methods that work before you.

Harvard innovation lab professor Michael Skok answers the question of how small companies can get big. It seems an easy question, but with a difficult answer. If you don't have a whole product solution end to end then learn to partner with a larger company and insert yourself in their value chain. What makes a partner strategic? When they can provide a greater benefit in growth and revenue to your small business than the cost. For example, 1+1>2. A big company will be motivated to work with a small company to complete their product chain because small companies price to be more innovative than big companies. Therefore by working with a small company, a big company can improve their margins and their time to market.

Skok goes on to say, as he looks at companies like Spotify and Airbnb, that we will see a new generation of entrepreneurs whose innovation is not a technical breakthrough, but instead is an innovative new business model. Meaning their product may be similar to another offering, but it is how they structure their business or deliver that product that will set them apart. Another side to this is to supplement your product offering by outsourcing or going virtual with some of the needs within your company that allow you to offer a full-service solution. You can drastically reduce cost and improve efficiencies by partnering with a virtual solution that knows that part of your value chain like none other.

In plain English, the lesson is this. Do not try to be all things to all people. If a product line does not fit your company's vision or cannot be produced cost effectively, then drop it. If you don't have the technological bandwidth to produce your product from end to end, find a vendor that can help with some of the steps. If your strengths are in one area of your business such as R&D or Sales, find someone to add to your team – either internally or through a virtual partner – to supplement the areas that are not your strong suit. You will not only increase the bandwidth of your small business, but you will increase your own longevity because your time will be focused on doing what you are good at and what you love.

4. Stay True to Your Beliefs

I meet with companies every week whose goal it is to gross $5 million, $50 million, $100 million and more. Will they stay true to their core beliefs as they approach that volume and beyond?

There are small businesses and there are big businesses. There are businesses that start small and become huge and then there are businesses that become huge and shrink again. And there is everything in between. The thought processes in a small business are much different than the thought processes in a large corporation. When does the brain of the company flip the switch from being the small business to being the big corporation?

And when you do become the company of your dreams no matter how large that may be, how do you stay true to your beginnings and provide the same consistent, wonderful experience to your customers and employees that got you there in the first place?

Establishing a culture with staunch firm beliefs early on is critical to setting the tone and building the culture that will carry on as your company grows. There are things that will change as you grow no doubt. If you are a CEO that personally checks in with each and every employee each week and you know all of their children's names when you have fifty employees, will you be able to also maintain that level of personal interaction when your company has ten thousand employees and they are spread out geographically? The answer is no. But a culture that permeates with a personal tone will allow you to empower managers and directors that work closely with those employees to bestow that personal touch and you can be the overarching voice of the company. This is not you becoming an impersonal CEO. It is you becoming the CEO of a larger corporation.

Your customer involvement will change too. As a small company, you can work directly with clients on projects. You can be involved in transactions in a much more detailed way. This may appeal to you or it may not. But something to consider as your company grows is that your time and availability are a finite resource. While customer service needs to be at the core of your focus, being the individual that personally handles transactions cannot be. By again being the overarching role model for what great customer service looks like, you can be farther removed, but still have customers that receive the same personal experience that they would with you.

Winning companies have a culture that you can cut with a knife. Stating your beliefs for your organization early and often is how a small business gets the momentum behind a culture that a large business can have. This is how you grow your company but still stay true to the beliefs that made you start the company in the first place.

5. Pick Your Battles

The transition from small to big while staying true to your vision and your beliefs is a difficult path. We gave the examples of McDonald's and Walmart as companies that have reached the pinnacle of growth in their industry, but there is a dark side to that tale as well.

Ray Kroc held the vision "Quality, Service, Cleanliness and Value" and kept that mantra at the core of the values of the company as it grew in size. Yet, in many circles, regardless of that mantra, McDonald's is one of the most hated corporations in the world. McDonald's is accused of a plethora of corporate sins including inhumane treatment of animals, contribution to landfills both with food packaging and toys, marketing of unhealthy food to children with a clown – you name it. They even got sued for their coffee being too hot.

Sam Walton promoted that people were at the center of his business. He called his human resources department the "people division". His passion was meeting the retail needs of the under-served rural population with less expensive products. In more recent news, Walmart has seen labor disputes in China over poorly disclosed store closures, and the chain has a long history of domestic battles with labor unions starting with the Retail Clerks International Union in 1970, the International Brotherhood of Teamsters in 1978, and the United Food and Commercial Workers International Union in 1999. Then, you've got the class action lawsuit alleging gender discrimination in 2001, "Operation Rollback" in 2003 where US Immigration officials raided 61 Walmart stores to remove illegally documented cleaning crew members, $172 million in damages paid to workers in 2005 for failing to provide meal breaks, over $800 million in damages between 2006 and 2008 related to unpaid hours of workers, and more into the following years.

Whether or not these companies are "good guys" or "bad guys" is not the point. The point is that no matter where your company ends up on the global stratosphere, you will probably piss some people off along the way. As a company grows, there will be angry customers, defective products, breakdowns in the systems, disgruntled employees, technology issues and maybe even lawsuits. A company simply cannot please all of the people all of the time. As your company grows, you will need to learn to pick your battles, shrug some minor things off and stay focused on what's best for the company. If you keep a valuable product, a supportive culture for employees and impeccable customer service within your core strategy, you will have fewer hiccups that take you off course and can learn to pick your battles as they arise.

6. *Learn From Your Mistakes*

As an entrepreneur, you're not going to know all of the answers the first time and you're going to make mistakes. You will encounter adversities on the road of being an entrepreneur. And that's okay. Entrepreneurs can have a lot of battle wounds and scar tissue. It is what allows you to get better and be smarter. An adversity can be a good thing if you learn from it.

Frank Wilczek is an American physicist born in the 1950s. He said "If you don't make mistakes, you're not working on hard enough problems. And that's a big mistake." Many products and services have come on the tail of a mistake or an adversity – penicillin, Silly Putty, potato chips, fireworks, Scotchgard, Corn Flakes, Post-it notes. All mistakes.

And adversities also go a big way toward moving entrepreneurs in a different – fruitful – direction. My firm's core virtual accounting product – VAST – started as the result of a restructure in my own firm that I at first saw as an adversity. It has now become my biggest opportunity. As we discussed in earlier chapters, thousands upon thousands of small businesses were started in the face of economic uncertainty and financial unrest.

Albert Einstein has been misattributed many times for supposedly defining insanity as doing the same thing over and over and expecting different results. Despite the true origin of the quote, this is still true. A product that doesn't change throughout its development is very rare indeed. Your products and your business will grow and evolve. You will make mistakes. Its learning from them that is important.

Go Big or Go Home

Small business statistics tell us that almost 80% of all small businesses fail. At the same time, even of those that succeed, the vast majority do not live past their original founder. The companies did not go from Garage to Great.

In companies that gain long term success and do maintain profitability, many can get stuck in the middle. The entrepreneur can find that after an early phase of aggressive growth, they can't get over the hump. Their sales stagnate, they find that they aren't meeting benchmarks set on the same path as historical results and they get stuck.

In many small businesses, one million can be a magical number. That first phase of growth – of reaching $1 million in revenues – can be the hardest. Whether your goal for your company is to reach that first million or many tens of millions beyond that or just to regain your sanity as an entrepreneur, this is where the concepts of

The Entrepreneurial Standard come into play. We will walk through strategies that you can put in place in your company to dramatically increase your bandwidth, the consistency of your product and the strength of your corporate culture – which in turn will fuel your growth.

Now, let's implement The Entrepreneurial Standard.

Chapter Four

THE ELF THAT WANTS TO BE A DENTIST

Hermey, the Misfit Elf

The Claymation Christmas special, *Rudolph the Red-Nosed Reindeer* that we grew up with first aired in the early 1960s. The North Pole is busy getting ready for the Christmas holiday. In the show, we meet Hermey – the misfit elf that wants to instead pursue a career as a dentist. We follow Hermey in his adventures with Rudolph as they meet many other misfits on the Island of Misfit Toys and all the while Hermey stays true to his real passion of dentistry. In the end, the elf supervisor allows him to open a dentist's office at the North Pole.

Large corporations have organizational charts and positions that are defined by those organizational charts. They have boards, committees and focus groups that can approve, research and proceduralize the best way to develop a product, solve a problem or accomplish a goal. Now, in the case of our hero, Hermey, the North Pole – being the large corporation –

broke from their organizational tradition in allowing him to venture out and pursue his dreams as a dentist creating a new business model that became a huge success at the isolated North Pole. There are two sides to this feel good tale – innovation versus organization.

The Spark of Innovation

On one side, a company can invest in a new venture allowing people within its walls to explore and develop new products, new ideas and new businesses. Hermey's innovation proved to be valuable at the North Pole and I'm sure his colleagues appreciate his practice. This is innovation.

Many companies encourage this type of innovation and have entire business lines or subsidiaries focused on developing new products and inventions. *Forbes* maintains an entire ranked list of the World's Most Innovative Companies each year. Players like Amazon, Starbucks, Salesforce and ninety-seven of their super innovative peers all have varying degrees of resources dedicated to exploring new ideas.

The top secret Google X innovation lab led by Astro Teller is fodder for a science fiction movie. Google has the reputation of being innovative anyway, but Google X takes that to a completely different playing field. Teller's title is Captain of Moonshots, which embraces the concept that there is a slim chance of success in some of the ideas they research but the effect they would have on the world would be profound if they did succeed.

John Hennessy, President of Stanford University, has an esteemed history rooted in entrepreneurship and technology. Hennessy speaks often about entrepreneurial leadership and how innovation is the crux of entrepreneurship.

Hennessy points out that innovation is the challenge that all small businesses, universities, and large businesses face. IBM grew very quickly when the mainframe was the computer of choice, but didn't grow as the personal computer or PC became popular. Now, PC companies don't grow as quickly because the Internet has become the driving force of technology.

The kind of entrepreneurial thinking that comes from understanding how to create innovation, nurture it, move it out and grow it is the key to building that innovative spirit. It begins and ends with people – people that have a vision that things can be done differently.

Stanford's heart and soul is its entrepreneurial way of thinking. Leland Stanford himself had a successful career as an attorney but then picked up his things and moved west. He found that a very successful venture was to start a mercantile that sold supplies to miners. After his retail accomplishments flourished, he then created the university.

Innovation can happen anywhere. Yahoo started in a couple of trailers piled with Coke cans and pizza boxes because Stanford had run out of classroom space. David Filo and Jerry Yang were two students working on a personal project that created simple lists of interesting websites. They then began to sort them by topical categories as the lists grew.

Not far away and a few years later, Larry Page and Sergey Brin started Google with the idea of doing library searches. The idea was to look up a book and rank the results based on the most relevant. What they found was that this translated to the Internet beautifully. It was basically a giant graph of popularity of search terms and this was the common algorithm that started Google.

The Problem as the Opportunity

Tina Seelig, Executive Director of the Stanford Technology Ventures Program, recently wrote a book entitled, *What I Wish I Knew When I Was Twenty.* Seelig teaches courses to entrepreneurs on creativity and innovation. She outlines that all problems are opportunities – the bigger the problem, the bigger the opportunity. All problems should be looked at through the lens of opportunity.

Vinod Khosla, founder of Sun Microsystems, echoes this sentiment stating that any big problem is a big opportunity. If there were not problems to solve, then there would be no solution to provide and thus there would be no company. Khosla emphasizes "Nobody will pay you to solve a non-problem." This is the core of entrepreneurship.

Teaching creativity can be difficult, but you can get people to be more innovative by getting them out of their comfort zone. It's not completely an intellectual experience. Seelig gives her students projects that definitely get them out of their comfort zone. A repeat project in her class asks students the question, "How much money could you earn with only $5 and two hours?" Each group is given an envelope that has an undetermined amount of money. They don't know up front that the envelopes contain only five dollars. They can plan as long as they want, but once they open the envelope, they only have two hours to make as much money as possible.

The teams that made the most money didn't use the five dollars at all. They realized that the five dollars was actually a limiting factor and that the five dollars was not important. They focused on their skill and what they could do regardless of the seed money they were given. One team set up a stand in the middle of campus. They said they would measure students' tire pressure for free, but if you needed air they would charge a dollar. Halfway through the experiment, they stopped asking for a dollar and started asking for donations instead. People started giving them more.

Another team realized that on Saturday night there were restaurants all over the city with long lines. They made reservations at all of these restaurants. As the time came up, they sold their reservations. The ones with buzzers made the most money. They could sell the buzzers they got a while ago to customers walking up, get a new buzzer and sell it later.

The team that made the most money realized that their most valuable resource wasn't the five dollars or the two hours, but that it was the three-minute presentation at the end where they presented their idea. They sold their company to someone that wanted to recruit them. Overall, the experiment proved that we often view a problem in too narrow a light.

Failures Are Opportunities for Innovation Too

In his presentation "The Biggest Successes Are Often Bred from Failures", Randy Komisar of Virtual CEO and Kleiner, Perkins Caufield and Byers, says about learning from failures that what distinguishes the Silicon Valley is not its successes but the way in which it deals with failure. He equates the technology industry to the earned run averages of major league ballplayers – they are going to strike out more than they hit home runs and they are probably going to hit less than 500.

Innovation is about taking risks to do things that haven't been done before. Entrepreneurship is the ability to tolerate failure, proceed with your career, learn from it and then cash in from what you've learned.

Staying Focused on Innovation

In his book *The Lean Startup*, Eric Ries talks about how he was given the opportunity to work closely with Intuit founder Scott Cook and CEO Brad Smith to learn about their focus internally on innovation. To this day Cook and Smith utilize entrepreneurial management within Intuit to maintain a keen focus on innovation and development of new products.

Intuit, the makers of such popular software packages as QuickBooks and TurboTax, holds themselves accountable for innovation within their company even now that they have become one of the largest software companies in the world. They measure to metrics to determine the relative value of their innovation efforts such as the number of customers using products that did not exist three years ago and the percentage of revenue coming from offerings that didn't exist three years ago.

Innovation is not just a luxury afforded the largest, most liquid companies in the world who have the budgets to set up James Bond-esque science labs in the Silicon Valley. Innovation should be viewed as lifeblood for your company's success. It is highly unlikely that you knew every product that your company would produce the very day you opened your doors. Even more unlikely is your ability to know exactly how those products and services will be perceived by the marketplace. It takes trial and error. It takes making mistakes and having failures. It takes learning from previous versions and improving on every rendition. It takes knowing your customers and constantly dedicating time and resources to innovation. Innovation is critical to growth in companies of all sizes, but it can't operate alone.

The Necessity of Organization

On the other side, there is the need for staying focused on the individual role that every team member plays without deviating from the plan. While Google X buzzes away with innovation and twenty-fourth-century inventions, the day-to-day life at the Google campus drones on. There is, after all, a business to run. What if every elf wanted to be a dentist like Hermey? Surely Christmas morning would be barren of toys. This is organization.

Staying true to the organizational chart is necessary for the day to day to get done. By focusing on developing an organizational chart for every role that the company needs to be at its best, you can ensure your organization will prosper. When creating your organizational chart, think of the characteristics, qualities and experience that the ideal person for that position would possess. Once the org chart is complete, you will draft a job description for each and every person in this new structure ensuring that all of the tasks needed to run your company are included in the job descriptions appropriately.

Small businesses frequently lack boards, do not have the resources to employ committees or focus groups and are much more likely to create a position that works for an individual they like rather than terminate that employee if they don't fit what the company needs. This is also true about pulling the trigger. Small businesses are much slower to fire than large corporations. Therefore, each existing team member should be evaluated for how their experience and personal strengths will be the best fit for the defined position while balancing the needs of the company.

Organizing Your Mastermind

While filling the positions within the organizational chart, evaluating the skills and personal traits that each individual brings to the table and contributes to the combined team is critical. Surround yourself with brilliant people and your team will be that much stronger. Napoleon Hill introduced his concept of the Mastermind in this *Law of Success*, published in 1928. The concept is based on principals of physics where synergy occurs between two like-minded individuals.

Go through the exercise of creating an organizational chart for your company to create the best and brightest team for your company, no matter how small or big you are now. The organizational chart should be based on tasks and responsibilities that need to be assigned and dovetailed into positions and roles that will need to be in place to get those things done when you reach your goal for the company's growth. For example, if your annual sales are currently $500,000 and you can accomplish that with five people, but your goal is to gross $5 million and you would need 35 people, then your organizational chart should include all of the positions that will be needed at $5 million. Of course, while you are still a team of five, a single individual would fill more slots on that organizational chart than they would at your goal. Once you are a larger company, the tasks that fill one position would be more likely to take a full employee rather than one employee wearing the hats of multiple positions.

This is very similar to the process Michael Gerber walks entrepreneurs through in *The E-Myth*. When a company is just starting out, the owners may fill all of the roles within the company. Defining who fills what role is critical so that the myriad functions within an organization are all handled and someone is accountable to them. Gerber recommends that the job descriptions be written in the format of a Position Contract. The person responsible for each position signs their name to the Position Contract that defines what they are responsible for. When a company is starting out, one person may be signing multiple Position Contracts. The important part here is in defining what those positions are and who is doing what. As the company grows, the Position Contracts can be migrated to new individuals that join the company. Ultimately, the organizational chart would have a Position Contract for every position and the ideal person for each position in each spot.

By balancing Innovation with Organization, you can ensure your company's growth while also keeping the foundation in place.

Chapter Five

PRESS 1 FOR ENGLISH, *PRESIONE 2 PARA ESPAÑOL*

Be Hard to Get Ahold Of

There is a phenomenon in small business that the owner or CEO must always be available. This open-door policy sounds good on paper and in brochures. In reality, it is murder to an entrepreneur trying to run a company, manage employees, market their products, keep customers happy, control financial resources, maximize profit and oversee internal processes. In order to accomplish all of this while not going completely mad, you need to be hard to get ahold of.

If you have a problem with an HP printer, do you call the current CEO of Hewlett-Packard, Meg Whitman, and demand she personally see to it that you receive compensation for your time and frustration? Of course not. And if you are brazen enough to actually appear at her offices demanding such justice, you will be handily escorted away by exceedingly large, possibly armed, security personnel.

When Windows 8 crashes yet again on my laptop, do I pick up the phone and call Bill Gates? When I want a pair of shoes from Zappos, do I have Tony Hsieh's personal email to send a message and have those shipped? When I fly Virgin Atlantic to London, is Richard Branson piloting the plane? It would be bad for them, the company and the stakeholders and probably you as the consumer if that were the case.

We discussed in Chapter Three how a business needs to stay focused on what it's good at. But what about you as CEO of your company? A CEO's role in a company – which is your role as an entrepreneur – needs to be focused on your personal sureties. What are the things in your company that only you can do? Here's an example: as an entrepreneur, you are the only person that can hold the vision for your company and where you want to go. What else? What are you spending your time on that you should not be?

The CEO of a large corporation, while their responsibilities are massive, has the luxury of separating themselves from many more processes than the small business CEO. It has become commonplace that an entrepreneur be readily available to all customers, vendors, employees and lenders. By following the lead of the large corporation CEO, an entrepreneur can find they are able to remove themselves from minutia and focus on their bigger role.

Now small business owners do not have the complete separation from day to day that the CEO's of multi-national, publicly held companies have. In fact, the entrepreneur has the even harder job of evolving into a more distanced role as the company grows rather than a large corporation's CEO who had that level of separation from the day they sign their HR paperwork.

In a company of five to ten employees, a customer often has a straight shot at the entrepreneur or CEO of that small business. If a customer called a small business owner with a complaint or concern, that entrepreneur could not say, "Let me transfer you to our customer service department and someone can help you." Something just as unlikely in a small business is that "Press one for English, Press two for Spanish" recording that you need to go through to get to a person. In many cases, small business CEOs are even easier to get ahold of than front line, entry-level customer service representatives in a large corporation! Obviously, in a small business that is growing, the answer lies somewhere in the middle of these two extremes.

Drop the Phone and Back Slowly Away from the Front Door

There is a slow weaning that takes place as a company grows. When your firm is still small, yes, you as the CEO need to field calls from everyone from customers to maintenance crews. As you grow, your personal involvement in the various aspects of the company diminishes, or should diminish, somewhat in proportion to that growth. You have to set clear boundaries in order to focus on your role in the company and you need to do this if you ever want to get anything done.

And, quite simply put, there are things that will be handled better by those complying with a system than you would as CEO of the company. I recently met with a retail client that is a friend of mine to review a price increase on his account and also do some tax planning. We spent some time catching up and talking about how as our businesses grew, the systems in place that our employees followed actually made our businesses more profitable. They would execute the processes more consistently than us rule-breaking entrepreneurs. When it came to the point of discussing his price increase I hesitated. He laughed and said, "Are you sure you don't want to get one of your people in here?"

You Don't Love Me Anymore

Now, not everyone will be as anxious to let go of you as in my example. Moving into this model must be done slowly. If you go too fast you will be surrounded by puppy dog eyes from customers and probably employees wondering what they did wrong and why they don't have full access to you anymore.

The ones that left after feeling neglected will shake their head slowly while explaining their plight to your competition that snatched up their business or your past employees. They will say "they simply grew too fast and weren't the same old company they used to be."

If they are saying that because you aren't effectively managing that growth and balls are getting dropped, then worry. Although you are removing yourself from personal involvement with every piece of every process, the customer and your team members should still receive the best your company has to offer them.

But, if they are saying that because you've grown and now have new processes in place to manage that growth and they will not be happy unless they have the direct dial number to the red phone on your desk, then you will need to be okay with that. This is a necessary part of your company's growth and your evolving role as CEO.

Make the Model Work for You

One strategy for putting in place these boundaries is using what I call the Car Lot Model. We've all been there – you deal with the smooth talking salesman on the lot who gets to play the role of being on your side. The salesman's job is to make you, the customer, happy. They get enough power to operate within a box of certain policies and procedures that the dealership has established.

You make an offer that you will pay X dollars for the vehicle. The salesman will respond with the typical response, which is, "Let me run that by my Sales Manager." This model takes any responsibility off of the salesperson for negotiating, and it also takes the pressure off of the Sales Manager to say no to your face. You will probably never talk to, see or meet the Sales Manager. The salesman in front of you has no power, and thus no responsibility. Undoubtedly, they will come back with some counter offer from the Sales Manager and shrug compassionately, saying that they can't do anything without their permission.

Granted, a small business owner will always be pulled into larger issues as they arise, but putting in place the Car Lot Model can help diffuse the volumes of disruptions the small business CEO gets and can improve other areas of your company as well.

A perfect example here is Accounts Receivable. Out of everyone in your company, you are the most likely to cave with a client when they need a little bit of leniency on payment terms and the customer knows that. Have someone else handle collections. Make them perceivable as the "powerless" car salesman that has to check upstairs to get the best deal. You can be that manager upstairs and separate yourself thus making your collections that much stronger. This not only saves you time, but it is better for the company financially.

Time Is Your Most Precious Asset

Entrepreneurs are the busiest people on earth. Beware of time vultures that will take that most precious resource from you. As an entrepreneur you will spend your day in the thick of your expertise, but you could also find yourself moonlighting as an accountant, a graphic designer, an attorney, a maintenance man, a peace ambassador and a therapist. Use your time wisely and remove anything from your day that doesn't help further your goals.

Dan Kennedy has written a series of managerial odes called *The No BS Guides*. His book *The No BS Guide to Time Management for Entrepreneurs* warns you to watch out for those time vampires. Be busy and be obvious about it to keep the time vampires from sucking you dry. "Do you have a minute?" is the opening line for time vampires that will destroy your productivity if you let them. Once they destroy your productivity, you and by default your company will never reach your goals. The multiple demands on an entrepreneur's time are nothing less than extraordinary. Which means time is your most precious asset.

Kennedy uses time management techniques like never answering his phone unless it's a scheduled meeting. He swears off of email and he makes it very hard for someone to get ahold of him. By doing this, he can ensure he is fiercely protective of his time.

Timothy Ferriss, author of *The Four-Hour Work Week*, also subscribes to guerrilla time management techniques. He has removed himself from many processes in his company that did not require his involvement. Email can be one of the biggest time vampires in a company. Tim Ferriss uses techniques such as only checking his email in a certain small window each day and when he does, responding to all emails in offline mode and sending them all at once so he doesn't end up in a volley back and forth with incoming emails. He even uses a virtual assistant to manage the first pass at all emails that come into his inbox. The VA then passes along only critical emails that Tim must answer – which is a very small percentage.

By protecting your time with the ferocity of a mamma bear protecting her cubs, you will allocate this vital resource wisely. You will also exponentially increase your bandwidth as CEO and take your company that much farther.

Pareto's Principle for CEOs

Pareto's principle is also known as the 80-20 rule or the rule of the vital few. It was first developed by Italian economist Vilfredo Pareto. It states that 80% of effects come from 20% of causes.

In business, this may sound familiar such as 80% of your sales come from 20% of your clients. On the flip side, it is common that 80% of complaints come from 20% of customers. You will have an easy move in a positive direction if you analyze the statistics in your company and determine where you can see the Pareto principle at work within your walls. Do 80% of your sales come from 20% of your sales people? Does 80% of your profit come from 20% of your staff's time?

As a CEO, you can use Pareto's principle to determine which processes to remove yourself from as your company grows. Do you, as CEO, get 80% of the results you need from 20% of your actions? Should you be involved in everything that you are currently doing? Identify the things that don't need you and where you are gaining the lion's share of results, and you can stay focused on the areas you need to stay focused on while enjoying the continued growth of your company.

Chapter Six

THE SYSTEM IS THE SOLUTION

When a company is just starting, it is very common to see the entrepreneur wearing many hats and completing lots of different tasks that CEOs of large companies do not involve themselves with. A new company needs to develop everything from scratch. The CEO could be involved in everything from developing a new product to drafting their very first employee handbook.

But, as we've seen, keeping a stranglehold on managing the minutia will quite literally cripple the growth of your company. This can come in many forms not the least of which are poor customer service, inconsistent products and a very stressed out CEO. You can't be that CEO that says, "But if I don't do it, who will?"

Systems not only free you up to accomplish more, they make your product and service more consistent. If you go to a restaurant once and have an amazing experience you will tell your friends. You will want to go back. If you go again and it's terrible, what will you decide is the real way that restaurant operates? And if you had the horrible experience the first time you went, would you have even tried it again? This is why systems are so important. And they affect everyone from the first person that interacts with that customer to the last.

When a company grows too quickly and doesn't have the systems in place to manage the growth, the company will begin to wobble as the maximum bandwidth of the entrepreneur is approached. Once the ceiling of what that CEO can involve themselves in is reached, the wheels basically fall off.

Putting in place systems within your organization is the closest thing you will get to cloning yourself. Each system is a detailed manuscript of how a particular process should be done. Systems can exist for everything from putting a stamp on an envelope to the quality control review of products before they go out the door. You create or oversee the committee or department that creates the system and then you train on the implementation and operation of that system. This guarantees both an increase in the capacity and upward potential of the company and a consistent repeatable customer service experience.

Sure, there are companies that didn't make it that had systems in place. The bottom line is this: If everything in your company is fundamentally strong (i.e., you have a good value proposition, a marketable product, a captive market, liquidity to fund the startup, etc.) then the systems will make all the difference. If you are lacking any one of those things, then all the systems in the world won't help. On the flip side, you can possess all of those traits and fail in an unorganized heap of personal and financial despair if you don't get organized about how it is you are going to run your company.

A Tale of Two Systems

There are processes that are done manually by employees and then there are systems that automatically handle many processes that were previously manual. Therefore, there are two types of systems that your business needs to have in place: 1) the systems that tell the people how to do things and 2) the systems that do it for them.

System 1 – The Wolf of Wall Street

In the 2013 blockbuster, *The Wolf of Wall Street*, the way that Leonardo DiCaprio's character, Jordan Belfort, was able to grow so quickly was because he provided a system that included a detailed script to every broker he employed. Every customer that was called received the same detailed script down to the very last word.

Every large corporation has this same type of scripted process in place. Whether you are calling tech support at a software company or calling to establish new service at the power company, the attendant on the other line will give you basically the same experience. They have a box in which they operate that addresses common requests and tasks in a customer interaction. It is so consistent that many large companies now employ voice-activated auto attendants to deliver the prepopulated Q&A instead of humans.

Consistency of experience is one of the biggest problems plaguing small businesses. Because small businesses are much less likely to invest the time and money in establishing documented, tested – and trained systems and procedures, there is much more learning by osmosis in a small company.

How consistent is the communication and the tone within your company? Your company should have established communication in place for as many processes as possible. Examples of this can be seen in customer service phone calls received by your offices, sales calls made to existing and potential clients, how employees answer phones and how services are implemented. It can even be something as simple as a standard format for signature lines in company emails.

By providing exact guidance on how to handle specific situations, the voice of your company remains consistent. Customers receive the same experience and your company looks like a larger corporation.

Internally, documenting the process for completing back of the house operations is just as important. How often have you had an employee leave only to panic on how you will train the next person on doing their job? Your operations manual should be an exhaustive play by play of all of the jobs it takes to run your company.

It can seem daunting in a small business to take the time and employ the resources to draft all of these lengthy procedures. But written policies and procedures provide a framework for your entire organization. Everyone wins when these are available in your company. As a business owner, you can control how an existing employee performs their duties and how a new employee is trained. With detailed procedures, if an employee is unsure how to complete a task, rather than make it up they can refer to the manual and not you.

The company can also communicate its policies – which include its philosophy, values and ethical standards – ensuring that all members of the team understand and subscribe to the company's vision.

System 2 – Automate, Automate, Automate

There are hard systems and there are soft systems. Both of which can be automated. Hard systems date back as far as Henry Ford's day when the assembly line model was developed. Modern manufacturing practices drive productivity growth in our economy. Everything from Jelly Bellies to Boeing 777s are the product of manu-facturing processes that streamline the development of the product.

Sure, manufacturing has been accused of decreasing employment growth by basically replacing people with machines. At the same time, the quality of manufactured goods continues to improve while the cost decreases thus improving the quality of life of Americans with better products that cost less. Manufacturing plays a vital role in the US economy and the industry itself demonstrates that the automation of a process is the major needle mover in a company's ability to expand.

Then there are soft systems. On the software side, companies are relying on technology at unprecedented levels and this will just continue to accelerate in the future. Entrepreneurs have an infinite number of systems at the ready to improve and streamline internal processes from billing customers to contacting leads.

A customer relationship manager or CRM system is becoming the norm in companies of all sizes. A CRM manages the marketing, sales and customer service side of your company and can often do so without much human involvement. The process of implementing a CRM system allows you to reduce the number of humans handling a process. This improves the response times in the process and also improves your bottom line by reducing labor cost.

CRM systems contain automated sequences that carry out a series of steps. What once was a manual process followed up on by sales people is now an automated chain of customer management, acquisition and retention. This allows a small business to free up the time of manually tracking and then completing menial marketing tasks such as a follow up email to a lead. With the CRM, the communication is automatic, consistent and thereby much more effective.

In 2013, we implemented Infusionsoft at my firm and dabbled in some minor campaigns to start. We replaced some of the mailings that went out and also changed the way we tracked recurring projects. We estimate that in the first year alone, Infusionsoft saved us over 3,000 labor hours. In a firm of just ten people at the time, this saved us hiring 20% more people! We basically replaced an employee and a half with about $4,000 in software cost. This is a significant flux to a small business. An automated system brings down the cost and also improves the experience not only for the customer but for the employees that no longer need to complete the menial tasks done by the system. Profitability, effectiveness and morale all improved.

Let Go

It can be common in a small business for the owner to have a difficult time stepping back from the day-to-day to focus on establishing these systems. In *The E-Myth*, Michael Gerber refers to this as working on your business rather than in your business. Small business owners spend their days on the front lines. They become ensconced in daily tasks. Unless they proceduralize their operation they will never be able to step back and have the faith that the system will carry on the same without them. With systems in place, the people taking over on the front lines will have the proper information to be able to do so.

Never before have there been so many systems and platforms available to the small business owner. This allows them to have the appearance and horsepower of a big company but also to streamline their systems so they can do more with less. It is vital for small businesses to run a lean and mean operation. But this can't come at the cost of looking unsophisticated. If a small business has collateral, websites or other outward appearances that look disheveled or not completely in sync, the client or outside party will not get the perception that your company has the expertise or the bandwidth to handle their project. Systems allow a small business to overcome this. They allow a small company to look big.

Fake it until you make it. But you're not really faking it. You're just systematizing it. By putting in place both proceduralized and automated systems, your company will enjoy consistency and efficiency, which will drive growth and profitability to new heights.

Chapter Seven

WHAT THE CABLE COMPANY TEACHES US ABOUT CUSTOMER SERVICE

Bugs Bunny and the Big Game

I recently watched a Bugs Bunny cartoon with my kids that showed Bugs trying to get his cable restored during the big game. Who of us hasn't had a frustrating encounter with a cable company?

"Thank you for calling Transvisitron, my name is Cecil, how may I offer you excellent customer service?" Cecil, the tortoise, is the Customer Service Rep at the cable company dripping with disdain who literally drives Bugs to the point of seeking retribution against the tortoise for what is no less than a horrific customer service experience.

Large businesses usually have pretty consistent customer service, but it may not necessarily be consistently good service. There are large corporations we deal with that we know going in are either going to provide an amazing experience or leave us grinding our teeth through a bad experience.

In an article in July 2014, *Forbes* magazine writer Caroline Mayer notes that people have become accustomed to or even expect poor customer service from certain industries such as telecommunications companies, health plan providers and airlines. While at the same time, investment firms, supermarkets and fast food chains have come to offer better customer service more frequently.

True to our cable company example, when children's cartoons and *Saturday Night Live* skits are poking fun at your industry's shoddy customer service, obviously it's pervasive.

Desperate times call for desperate measures. To be heard at some large corporations, when there is bad customer service, you have to scream louder. Fight harder. Large corporations can often act as if they are too big to be bothered with things like great customer service. Those that do aim to set themselves apart invest huge sums both in hard cost and in internal capacity to ensure that they remain exemplary.

Customer Service Legends

More has been written about outstanding customer service than probably any other topic in business. Some of my favorite customer service stories come from companies that offer world renowned customer service that you can feel from the moment you enter their doors. The first that always comes to mind is Ritz-Carlton.

Simon Cooper, past president of The Ritz-Carlton Hotel Company, wrote the foreword to Joseph Michelli's book *The New Gold Standard – 5 Leadership Principles for Creating a Legendary Customer Experience, Courtesy of the Ritz-Carlton Hotel Company.* As he started his role as president of the Ritz-Carlton hotel chain, the first phenomenon he encountered was the consistency of devotion and genuine service from the highest managers to the front line staff. Whether an individual was running the property or running the washing machine, the words "That's not my job" were noticeably absent in the vocabulary of the team. The "Ladies and Gentlemen" of the Ritz-Carlton Hotel Company demonstrated a sincere care and unyielding dedication to the company and to its guests. He refers to a conversation overheard in a hallway with an employee and a guest where the employee stated "The answer is Yes, now... What is the question?" Over the top customer experiences like this demonstrate the importance of outstanding service from every level within your organization.

The Nordstrom Way to Customer Excellence: The Handbook for Becoming the "Nordstrom" of Your Industry and *Be Our Guest: Perfecting the Art of*

Customer Service (The Disney Institute) tell the stories of how both Nordstrom and Disney offer their guests outstanding, polished experiences from the moment they step through their doors. These are not small companies. But they have meticulously perfected not only the customer service aspect of their business, but making their service define in part who they are as a company, allowing them to stand alone in their industries. By following their lead, you will in turn ensure that you also set your business apart.

Shampoo, Rinse, Repeat

Small businesses must offer consistently better customer service in order to stay competitive and grow and they must do all of that with more limited resources. But, small businesses are much more likely to have inconsistent customer service than large businesses. An inconsistent experience can be just as deadly as a bad one. The consumer is usually much more forgiving of a horrible experience from the large chain, than the mom-and-pop. This is why it's critical for an entrepreneur to remain keenly focused on providing great service, ensuring consistency of experience and using resources devoted to customer service and business development as efficiently as possible. Not an easy task for the entrepreneur to undertake.

Consistency of experience is a common denominator in large companies with world-class customer service reputations. They have crystallized how to empower employees so that the same great customer service that is received from the CEO of the company is experienced at every level within the organization. It is as predictable as the instructions on a shampoo bottle – "Shampoo, Rinse, Repeat."

Your organization must embody great customer service at every level – and consistency from experience to experience – from the first interaction to the last. In a small business, the business owner or entrepreneur has great customer service skills – often being the best sales person on the force. If you as the entrepreneur embody a passion and general excitement for your clients but then the experience your customer has once they don't deal directly with you, leaves them feeling deflated, this will result in lost business. Losing a client and going and getting a new client to replace them uses much more of your time and energy than providing an excellent experience and keeping that client in the first place.

Sure, customer service also has a lot to do with price point – to say that Ritz-Carlton and Nordstrom have great customer service is like saying that there is sand at the beach. You will not get the same customer service experience at a Nordstrom that you get at Kohl's. Just like you won't get the same customer service at a Ritz-Carlton that you get at a Courtyard by Marriott – even though the two are owned by the same parent company.

Who Are Your Customers?

Your customer service focus changes dramatically based on the answer to this question. Focusing on the makeup of your client base and expectations versus results can be a major force in your customer service culture.

Specific advice on customer service protocol and marketing strategy is outside the scope of this book and I definitely do not purport to be an expert on either. Whether it is conversion rates, social media presence, online marketing, email opt-ins, customer relationship management software, e-commerce structure and on and on – the myriad of terminology and options can be mind-boggling. I enlist an army of experts to navigate these waters for me. But what I do know is that knowing your customer – who they are and how they interact with your company – can help you decide which experts, strategies and forums to put in play in your company's strategy and how to allocate resources effectively – in short, what works and what is a waste of time.

By understanding your Business Development Gap, your Client Base and your Client Lifetime Value – three topics we will cover here – you'll be able to provide consistent wonderful experiences to your customers, improve customer retention and make that small business dollar go even farther.

1. The Business Development Gap

What is your goal for your company's revenue? Do you know how you're going to meet that goal or how far you are above or below it?

The Business Development Gap is the difference between revenue you have already booked and your goal for gross revenues during the same period. If you plan for your company to have a million dollars in revenue and you know that you already have signed contracts for $300,000, you know that you have to go get the rest of those orders – or $700,000 in additional sales. This is your Business Development Gap.

When analyzing your Business Development Gap, you must break that down into any divisions or product lines within your company too. Say that you have a company that manufactures nuts and bolts. You have a factory full of machinery and employees ready to fulfill orders for both – one for nuts and one for bolts. If you've already filled enough orders to keep the bolt factory running at full capacity all year, while the nut factory has hardly enough orders to keep everyone busy, you need to make a decision. Do you reallocate resources over to the bolt factory internally to keep the bolt orders flowing? Or do you focus your marketing dollars on bringing in more orders for nuts? You need to focus on which part of your Business Development Gap to address – more nut orders or more bolt capacity.

If yours is a recurring revenue model and you can retain clients from year to year with minimal attrition, then you can move closer and closer to that budgeted revenue amount with sales that are already on the books at the start of each year. However, if yours is a model where you must go get new clients every year because you only sell to a given client once or they don't buy your products for several years at a time in between purchases, then you must climb back into that hamster wheel every month or year and drum up new business in order to cover your Business Development Gap. This is where knowing your Client Base comes in.

2. Your Client Base – Devotees vs New Blood

Once you establish your goal for your company's revenues within a given year, knowing your Client Base and how your customers interact with your company is vitally important to the growth and strong profitability of your small business. How much of your business is made up of devotees – meaning recurring business – versus new blood – meaning one time or infrequent purchases? This is the difference between customer service and marketing. Great customer service will keep your customers coming back. But if your client base is not made up of repeat business or if your company is growing and you need to bring in new business to meet your goals, then your focus would be on marketing to new leads instead.

It is critical to provide great service as a means to an end of retaining clients and gaining referrals, but the makeup of your customer base as either recurring or new changes the way you serve that client base. If a large portion of your client base is recurring, your focus is primarily on client retention. In order to grow, you must first retain the clients you have and then seek to find new ones. It is much harder to find and sell to a new client than to keep an existing customer. In order to make your small business dollar and your time-strapped hour stretch farther, retaining your clients with superior products and wonderful customer experiences will keep customers coming back at a higher rate.

An example of this could be a grocery store. People buy groceries frequently each and every week. A logical focus would be on customer loyalty and getting customers coming back with competitive pricing and great service. Losing your existing client base because of poor service or lack of attentiveness will keep you spinning your wheels and inhibit your company's growth.

No matter how great you are at customer retention though, every year every business loses a percentage of revenue and customers. Whether it is that they no longer need your product, that they found your product elsewhere, or that they received less than stellar customer service, customers move. Revenue leaves. The simple truth is that your new customers and revenue must exceed your lost customers and revenue if you are to grow. Bringing in revenue to just replace the attrition each year will keep you in the same place.

If yours is a business where your customers buy your product once or very infrequently, you need to keep current customers happy, but the crux of your revenue is in bringing in new work. A home builder would be an example of this type of business. People don't usually buy a new house every day or month. So, a home builder must constantly be looking for new customers.

Another focus should be on where you find your customers. In our grocery store or homebuilder example, unless yours is a mail order grocery store or you are a national real estate developer, a company in Austin, TX, would not spend their marketing dollars trying to attract clients in Seattle. This sounds like a silly example on the surface, but small businesses have more of a tendency to not do thorough research of where their customers are coming from and thus are not marketing to the right people. Make sure you are getting the most bang for your buck in how you allocate your customer service and marketing dollars. Poor use of resources can be more costly in a small business where resources need to stretch even farther than in a large corporation.

3. Your Client Lifetime Value

Every company with every type of customer base should know their Client's Lifetime Value. A grocery store with a recurring client base should understand over an average span of a customer's lifetime of visits to their store the total value that the client represents in sales. This would be expressed as average number of years a customer stays times number of visits per year times average sale per visit.

A homebuilder that builds a home for a client either one time in their lifetime or only once after many years would have a larger per transaction value, but that transaction would only happen once or a few times. This would be expressed in terms of number of homes a client would purchase during their lifetime times the average value of the home. Obviously, these are estimates, but it gives you a strong perspective into how your clients operate and if you are consistent in how you calculate these factors, you will be able to see and measure trends in your company over time.

Do you know the lifetime value of your client? This is different for every company. For a firm like mine, the lifetime value includes monthly accounting, maybe yearly tax work and often some additional consulting. Ours is a repeat customer model. If I bring in a single client and we can demonstrate superior service, the lifetime value of that client will reach far beyond my revenue goal for the current year. That client will contribute to my company's revenue for years to come.

But what about a real estate agent or car dealer? How often does a client buy a larger purchase like a car or a home? And how many will they buy in their lifetime?

As your company grows, you can make the decision of how your company's customer service evolves. Keeping the tone consistent throughout your organization will no doubt help you reach your goals. But taking the time to truly analyze your Business Development Gap, Your Client Base and breakdown of your customers between recurring and one-time purchase, while also estimating your Client's Lifetime Value, can help you gain a better understanding of the service areas that will more easily propel your business toward its goals.

Scalable Customer Service

An entrepreneur is intimately involved at the customer experience level when their business is small. Each and every customer interaction is a reflection on their personal hospitality, quality and service. This is of course not sustainable if you want your company to grow. While you want your customers to have the best experience possible, being the sole individual capable of making that perfect experience a reality is a recipe for complete and utter failure. The only way to absolutely control the customer experience and to be the only person responsible for providing that experience is to keep your operation so small that you as an individual can handle every aspect from start to finish of the lifetime value cycle of your clients.

For some, this is perfect. They want to stay small. Stay hands on. Be involved with every customer interaction that occurs under their roof. This is a great business model for those that choose this route. Not every entrepreneur wants to scale their company to great heights, gross tens of millions of dollars, deal with the headaches of multiple locations, dozens of employees, the additional overhead. And all is good. These companies make up a noticeable portion of the small businesses in the United States. They may or may not set themselves up to be acquired or taken over when the original owner wants to retire. In some cases, a son or daughter may take over the reins and keep the family business going. There are thousands of local institutions that are family-run companies taken over from generation to generation that carry on with consistent quality and service. These are the companies that pioneered the systematic delivery of a consistent product. These are not staff that read a personnel manual or a standard operating procedure. This is a practiced craft that is carried down through the ages that is lovingly taught in enough detail to ensure consistency of product and experience regardless of whether you are dealing with the founder, their son or their great-great-granddaughter.

On the flipside, a large corporation can have customer service amnesia. The experience is not a legacy at all. I remember an incident with a large utility company. I had a horrible experience with a representative after they lost more than two months of payments that I had sent in. I swore off of them for good. Weeks or months later, I received a letter with an offer that was way too good to pass up. Did I question it? No. Did I think, "My gosh! Don't they realize what a bad experience I had with them last month?" No. I signed up again.

This is an amazing large corporation phenomenon. Small business owners are far less likely to reach out to attempt to re-sign customers that had stopped working with them in the very recent past. Customers of a small business hearing from the CEO of that small business with an offer to re-up would probably think that the entrepreneur should be committed. You see, when a small business reaches out it is viewed as a personal connection. When a large corporation reaches out, it is par for the course, accepted as one hand not talking to the other, and viewed as part of an automated marketing campaign.

To an entrepreneur, customer service can be a very intimate experience. If you have a good or bad experience with a small business, you associate that good or bad experience with the entire organization. And, most commonly, it's personal.

Somewhere in the middle lies the answer. Scalable customer service means that as your company grows, the experience at every level remains consistent and personalized. You can create a culture that employs the best practices of the customer service experience you want to create – such as the tradesperson handing down their secrets to the next generation – and also ensure your company's growth – by ensuring that all ranks within your company understand the procedures, culture and tone that you want your company to embody.

Pruning the Rosebush

Pruning is necessary as a small business grows. Just as one would prune a rosebush to ensure a more beautiful healthy plant and more blooms, you must prune your client base to clients that help you achieve your mission within your company. Sometimes a client taxes such resources or poses such a liability that they must be cut from the rosebush.

When I first started my firm, I read an article about a managing partner that had some problem clients within his firm. He circulated a client list to his personnel and asked that they highlight any clients that they felt should be terminated from the firm based on the way they treated the staff members, the amount of resources they absorbed, their understanding of the value of the services provided and so on. In the end, the staff recommended clients for termination that represented approximately 10% of the firm revenue. The managing partner kept his word and terminated the troublesome clients based on the recommendations of the team. In the following year, the firm filled not only that 10% with better clients that respected and valued the relationship but actually increased overall firm revenue by 30%.

However, this pruning decreases as a company grows. It's not that big companies don't need to prune out nightmare, loss leader clients. It's just that as a company becomes more sophisticated in its systems and culture, the "bad" clients can take less of a toll on the company. The CEO is more separated from the client and the procedures ensure that they are dealt with in a consistent, arm's-length way.

I don't think the CEO of AT&T labors over the decision to terminate me as a client when I turn into Sybil while dealing with a customer service representative. The system handles the issue. The client relationship is fed into the machine and issues are escalated according to the customer service playbook. Employing these systems in your company as you grow allows your front line to deal with the troublesome clients that used to be escalated directly to you when your company was small.

Chapter Eight

MAKE BIG DECISIONS

What Scares and Excites You

There is a time and a place for bootstrapping. Every entrepreneur has done it. But bigger balances in your bank accounts allow you to make bigger decisions. Think about Coke or Pepsi.

In 2013, a Super Bowl ad of thirty seconds was running about $4 million. A cultural phenomenon in and of itself. Do you think the executives that placed that ad considered that a big decision? Did it scare them to make that decision?

Entrepreneurs don't make decisions like that. As an entrepreneur, you may have to decide between sweetening the employee benefit pot and putting more dollars into online ads. Those amounts could be big or they could be small relatively speaking, but it's all big to you! Not so much with the Director of Marketing at a large conglomerate that drops a cool $5 million on that next Super Bowl ad!

There is a change that happens with what scares and excites you as you grow and continue to expand your outer boundaries. When something scares and excites you that's a great thing. It excites you because you want it. You have made the decision to get it and you will also make decisions that will make getting it a reality. It scares you because it is a stretch outside of where you are right now. When I first started my firm in 2002, what scared me was completely different than what scares me now. As you grow, as your company grows, you will expand and new things will scare and excite you. You will make big decisions in order to make big strides toward what you ultimately want. What would you love to see in your future? And what big decisions do you need to make to get there?

Bootstrappers Unite

An entrepreneur is much more likely than a large corporation to bootstrap their operation. With the trend toward small business financing drying up, bootstrapping became the only option many small businesses had – like it or not. Bootstrapping means that an organization is funded solely on its own through a combination of capital contributions by the owners as they can afford them, reinvestment of net income from operations as it is collected and keen, almost militarian, control of expenses.

I am a huge fan of bootstrapping. I think it possesses many benefits, not the least of which is an intimate knowledge of how your company makes and spends its money. It also allows the buck to stop with you. A bootstrapping mindset means that you are still privy to the information you need to have about your company's inner workings. A bootstrapping mindset becomes less about the actual dollars and cents and more about the concept of your involvement as CEO in the day-to-day operation of your company. With an intensive bootstrapping mindset comes the risk that you aren't able to make those big decisions because of a stranglehold on the minutia.

Focus on a balance between the two – keep a healthy bootstrapping mindset while also making the big decisions that will affect your company's ultimate outcome. Stay knowledgeable in the things that make your company tick. Do not relegate ultimate responsibility to someone else. You need to stay in the driver's seat and while you will step back from smaller details – don't be ignorant of clues that you sense in how your company is driving. If you sense that there is something wrong in how your company is operating, it is up to you to have the working knowledge to investigate it and avoid careening off course. It is inexcusable to me when I hear about large corporate CEOs that plead ignorance and play dumb when their companies crumble and shareholders lose billions – sometimes their entire life savings.

The most famous situation is Enron. How is it that their CEO Kenneth Lay could sign and review financial statements and tax returns, sitting through thousands of hours of board meetings and committee meetings where decisions were made and documents were signed, and then claim no knowledge of any of it? It doesn't fly. Whether he was telling the truth about his ignorance or not, it is expected that a CEO be more knowledgeable than that. And the courts agreed. So he was sentenced to prison and actually died of a heart attack before serving a day behind bars.

Enjoy the Silence

Being able to pull the trigger and make big decisions when needed will separate your company from those that were unable to scale and grow. You can keep your finger on the pulse of your ultimate goal while seeing the forest for the trees. Sometimes it is just giving yourself the luxury of silence in order to think and determine the best course of action.

One night recently, the power went out at our house. I had just sat down to start that "second shift" that every entrepreneur knows about after the kids have gone to bed and the chores are done. The power usually doesn't go out for more than a few minutes these days with the new technologies that keep us continuously, mercilessly connected in everything we do. But with the wind and new snow approaching that night, the power stayed off for an hour or two.

At first, I had the immediate response that most of you would have: the "Oh, crap!" moment; the "I really, really, REALLY needed to get caught up!" moment. I paced around the house lighting candles and grabbing every connected device with a battery. But then I paused.

The only conceivable sound in the house was the beep of the battery backup in our home office. Other than that, there was silence. And, I may add, quite serene from the myriad of candles burning in order to light the way for another late night of work on an iPad, phone or anything else that didn't need electricity.

What did I do? I sat still. I mean, really sat still. And it was awesome. Never underestimate the power of time dedicated to thought. But, with the onslaught of demands on a business owner, the crescendo of chaos can rise to a fever pitch to the point that you become desensitized. You are numb to it. This desensitization is detrimental to your company.

There was a man named Dr. Elmer Gates that lived in the post-Depression era. Dr. Gates held over 200 patents with the US Patent Office. He would sit in a room he called his "personal communication room" with basically a table, a pad of paper and a switch for the lights. He would sit in this room, turn off the lights and ideas would "flash" in his mind through his Creative Imagination. His method was so proven that Dr. Gates earned a substantial living "sitting for ideas" for fees from some of the largest corporations in America.

Make time to sit still. Channel the ideas that are just below the surface if you just gave yourself a chance to think about them. You will be amazed at the answers you already have.

It's Not the Dog in the Fight, but the Fight in the Dog

As we've seen, there are certain things that scare a small business owner more than the CEO of a large corporation. One of those things is a legal battle. I'm not just referring to a full blown lawsuit, but any sort of legal wrangling, client dissatisfaction beyond what a customer service manager can smooth over or violations of any sort of standard or rules that govern your type of business. But these legal issues have a way of becoming less daunting in scope the more war wounds you possess. I have spoken with a key group of very successful entrepreneurs that have faced very drastic material adversities in the history of their company or their career. Not one has said that given what they know now, they would have responded the same way that they did then. When you are first faced with something like a lawsuit, an investigation or some other huge battle in your company, it can be a terrifying experience. I know. I've been there. I dealt with it in my own firm, I saw my husband go through a horrific jury trial brought about by a lunatic in his business, and I have seen clients near and dear to me stare down a courtroom set on destroying them.

The profound effect that something like this can have on a business owner and the direction they will subsequently take their business is not something to brush over lightly. It is not possible to complete a surface-level chapter on the mental strength it takes to be an entrepreneur. In talking to these entrepreneurs and recounting my own legal battle, these were terrifying recollections about how your livelihood, your profession and the sheer core of what you as a professional represent to the consumer world, can be violently shaken.

But let's look at the lawsuit example a little more closely. Actually, let's use just the threat of legal action because very, very few threats actually become full-blown lawsuits. The reality is that in business sometimes people just don't get along. There are disagreements. There are threats. There could be legal action. This is not the end of the world and you will live. It may be unpleasant, but it will eventually be over.

The more battle-worn entrepreneurs will be able to differentiate between that first legal encounter, which actually can feel like a personal assault, and any subsequent adversities, which will seem less dramatic and daunting. The irony is that of all of the people I know, myself included, that had some sort of legal settlement, lawsuit or regulatory issue, they all across the board said that if they had to do it over again they would not have settled so easily, agreed to as much or given up as much.

Unfortunately, the first experience with something like this can be so utterly terrifying that you may end up settling for something horrific just because knowing is much better than not knowing and the fear is so great that it is worth it to have closure.

Adversity reveals innovation, strength, wisdom and courage. It reveals products on countless occasions that never would have been discovered if their creators had experienced nothing but smooth sailing. Adversity does not create character. It reveals it.

Do not view adversities or failures as a bad thing. In order to have success, you must have failures. Do not under any circumstances compare yourself to peers thinking that if you had just avoided the adversity you would be ahead of where you are. It doesn't work that way. The adversity was necessary to get you where you are.

Adversity is the key to opportunity and future success. If I had not suffered an adversity in my professional life that caused me to redirect the purpose and values of my firm, you would not be reading these words right now.

Sacrifices that Pay Off

When I graduated from high school, I immediately started college. Throughout college, I worked in various accounting positions. I had bosses that took me under their wing to varying degrees – seeing something in my tenacity and hunger that made them want to give me projects and assignments that were above and beyond what my then textbook education would support. I started to learn that this thing called accounting came naturally to me and that I could be creative and strategize with the numbers to make them more useful for the end users of that information. I really loved what I was learning but I was flat broke.

At about the same time, I had a high school friend who decided to go straight from high school into a government job. This was the very early nineties and she was immediately making a strong hourly rate of $14 then $16 then $18 per hour. This was a lot of money to us at the time. I was working in an entry-level accountant position for a humbling $7 per hour. I didn't have my degree yet, and I desperately wanted large corporate experience so I gladly accepted this meager wage and worked diligently and lots of hours trying to keep up with the demands of the job. My friend had a full benefits package. I had tons of overtime. While she made over double what I did, I not only worked that initial accounting job but also took four undergraduate classes and cleaned two offices at night to make ends meet. I slept less than five hours a night trying to juggle the demands of two jobs, studying and learning my profession. She spent her spare time playing trivia during happy hour at TGI Fridays.

I worked my way up through the ranks. I was able to move from the entry level position into a position under the CFO handling special projects like construction in process and inventory. When I started at this large company, I worked in payroll. While I was there, the payroll manager and I streamlined the department to be half the employees and shortened the time it took for department heads to receive their payroll reports by two days. The company had over 2,200 employees and, back then, every single employee's payroll information had to be entered by manually data entering every single social security number and their total hours into a proprietary AS400 system every single week. I worked my way up from the early \$7 to \$8 and then \$9 per hour – and it was earned cent by painstaking cent per hour. After years of criticism from my so-called friend for not bellying up to the bar with her and our other friends for trivia night, making hardly enough to pay my rent, and sleeping barely enough to function in college, I was finally making progress.

This journey was my big decision to make. I knew that this would lead to big things. I was the first in my entire extended family to graduate from college and I knew I was making the impossible possible.

Since those early days, I started and grew my company and have over a dozen years under my belt in my current role. I have made many, many bigger decisions since then. Whether it was bootstrapping my way through college or the start of my company until we met with success, the bootstrapping mindset has been part of my journey as long as I can remember and I wouldn't have it any other way.

Getting in the Zone

You know when a decision is a good one. You can feel it. Everything is working and you are firing on all cylinders. You know when a decision is a bad one. It's like a bad relationship. When you feel like you always say the wrong thing, trip over your own dress, make a fool out of yourself. You are not in the zone. When you are, you say the right things and things work out.

By becoming an entrepreneur, you are making the impossible possible. You are prepared to do whatever it takes. To go big. So, how did a girl from Carson City who was the first in her family to graduate from college and who grew up cleaning office buildings create a company that allows her to manifest all of the things that she wants to see in her life both personally and professionally? There is a fine line between the life I've created that includes teaching an international audience of entrepreneurs from numerous stages and working with clients all over the United States and in seven countries versus those early days where I was struggling for a meager existence while working my tail off to make my goals a reality.

The secret ingredient to me would be grit. It is staying true to your vision while kicking ass and taking names. And I'm not the only story like this. I speak with devoted entrepreneurs constantly that show their mettle while balancing work, life and superhero status.

Linda Rottenberg, CEO and co-founder of Endeavor Global, wrote the *New York Times* bestseller *Crazy Is a Compliment*. She explains that the hardest backer you will ever have in your business is you. Do you think you're crazy for doing what you're doing? If the answer is yes, then Rottenberg's answer back is that is why you're going to succeed.

Rottenberg goes on to say that the first part of doing anything different is being misunderstood. Because if you're trying to shake up the status quo, those following the status quo are not necessarily going to embrace your vision. Once you embrace your decision to be different, brace yourself. Because everyone else is going to criticize your choice. Turbulence is the official climate of entrepreneurship.

Where do you want to go? Where do you see your company landing on the Garage to Great continuum? If your answer is I don't know, then get a plan, get a vision and focus on that more intently than anything you have ever visualized in your entire life. Keep your finger on the pulse of your company and make the big decisions to set yourself apart.

Chapter Nine

THE ENTREPRENEURIAL STANDARD AT WORK

Run for Your Life

There is an Aesop's fable that I still remember from my childhood called "The Hare and The Hound." It goes like this. A hound spotted a hare and gave chase. After some distance the hound began to gain, but then gave up the chase. As the hound returned home a farmer commented that the little hare had been too much for the hound, who replied, "It's one thing to run for your dinner, but quite another to run for your life." We have a higher chance of success when our job, career or livelihood depends on it.

Entrepreneurship is a phenomenon. Being an entrepreneur is about solving a problem and making something from nothing. Entrepreneurs are that hare running for its life – that's why only about 13% of people do it, according to the *2012 Global Entrepreneurship Monitor (GEM) U.S. Report* issued by Babson College and Baruch College. What does it mean to be an entrepreneur and what does it take? Some say it takes a combination of grit and street smarts. Others say it is all about creating your own luck or at least insulating yourself from bad luck by creating your own economy. Nonetheless, it seems very ethereal. How does one learn to be a truly great entrepreneur other than being born with an innate sense of intuition toward such? Entrepreneurship is not really something that can be taught – although there are plenty of college and high school level courses touting to do just that. Entrepreneurship is a state of mind and a level of tenacity. It's deciding how to be proactive, while being efficient and while being profitable. It's more of a cult than a class. Being an entrepreneur is a badge of honor. Anyone who is an entrepreneur is proud to announce it. If they aren't, then they aren't a true entrepreneur.

You've seen in the chapters of this book that entrepreneurship is a vital force in the building of this nation's economy. Entrepreneurs will find an opportunity where there is a need. I recently went to the post office to renew passports for my children. Every single person in line was handily turned away to go get additional copies of various forms of identification. Because everyone was turned away, it was easy to assume that it wasn't that a single person had failed to follow the instructions outlined on the USPS website. It was a breakdown in the instructions. But when each person approached the counter, the standard response they received was to go next door to the mini market and get additional copies of identification, whether it was a driver's license or a passport. If you contested those instructions and asked to have the postal worker instead make the copy, they would impatiently explain that it was literally against the law for them to collect money and make the copy for the customer.

So it was that each customer made the same pilgrimage – stand in line, get turned away, walk next door to mini mart, make copies, return to line. The owner of the mini mart needs to be congratulated for recognizing an opportunity that they are now able to capitalize on. And the most amusing part of watching all of this from my place in line was that the post office was literally doing all of the store's marketing for them by sending everyone right to their door. While the post office keeps raising the price of postage cent by cent, the mini mart owner has most likely seen a marked improvement in top line revenues.

The Fallacy of Limited Wealth

There is another story that I love and it's about a chicken farmer. This farmer explained how she would go into the large pen that was outside her chicken coop carrying a large tray overflowing with food for the hens and put it down in the middle of the area. It was a pretty big area – say 12 by 20 feet – and all of the chickens would run into the farthest corner when she walked into the pen. She would put down the tray and only the bravest of the chickens would venture forward to this platter overflowing with food. They would steal some scraps, load as much into their mouth as possible, and then they would run back into the farthest corners of the pen. Now the other chickens, the less brave, less wise chickens, rather than approaching this overflowing platter in the middle of the pen, would chase down the ones who had the food, clawing savagely at the scraps hanging from their mouths. All the while they didn't even realize that right behind them there was an overflowing platter that would feed them all to their hearts' content. This epitomizes the fallacy of limited wealth.

Limited wealth implies that there is only so much to go around – that there is only so much prosperity, there is only so much success, and there is only so much money to go around. I'm not talking about the kind of money that is finite like money that is in your wallet or the kind the government can print more of if we find ourselves in debt. I'm talking about the wealth that you can create from an idea or opportunity in your business or personal life.

There is a common belief that the world has a balance sheet. That if wealth exists in the world there are assets, there are liabilities, and there is a limited amount of wealth to go around. Under this premise, if you were to take the people in the world and divide that wealth, there is a set amount and it will all add up to the same even if it moves from one hand to another.

In reality, life has no balance sheet. What about the wealth that is created from thin air? What about the wealth that disappears into thin air? In the recent recession, wealth vanished. Stocks went down. Real estate values went down. Wealth vanished into thin air. But at the same time, there were companies that were created. Business owners that were passionate about the growth of their ideas that pursued their dreams even though there was a recession going on. Many of these entrepreneurs have been more successful than they even imagined they could be. Their sales grew, their stock price grew, and wealth was created from thin air. This demonstrates that ultimate global wealth can shrink and or grow as things are either created or devalued.

There's a skit that David Letterman does on his late show that talks about where the money has gone. He said that all of these values dropped and he wants to know where it went. "Where is that money? Who's got that money?" In most cases, it's not that someone has it. It's that it was either created or it no longer exists. If you have a share in a company that's worth ten dollars a share and that company's value went up to twenty dollars a share and you have ten shares – you now have two hundred dollars as opposed to one hundred dollars in your possession. With regard to that one hundred dollars in additional value, no one cut you a check for that. No one gave you clam shells or diamonds or corn or any other medium of exchange for that. You now have one hundred dollars more wealth than you did before. This is evidence that wealth can expand or contract based on what we can produce. And there's really no upward limit to what you can produce as an entrepreneur. Look at Facebook. Look at the billions of dollars in wealth that was created by the generation of an idea or a product. The wealth that entrepreneurs can create from something they're passionate about or a company they create is infinite. It is absolutely infinite.

Remember those chickens. It may feel like you need to go and take market share, and all of the statistics say that you need to fight for market share. That's what those chickens are doing when they're fighting for scraps hanging from their peers' mouths. They're fighting for market share, because they believe that market share is finite. What if we look back at that platter that's overflowing in the middle of the bin, and we realize that wealth and opportunity are not finite?

In reality, entrepreneurs create their own economy. I don't want to spend my life fighting over the scraps hanging from some other chicken's mouth and I know you don't either. Go back to that platter. Rather than the scraps that you can steal from someone else's mouth, find the infinite bounty, the infinite prosperity, and the infinite abundance that you can create if you focus on your own growth and your own ideas, your own passion, inspiration and innovation.

The Superpower of Entrepreneurship

The Kauffman Foundation is the world's leading foundation for entrepreneurship. It was established in the 1960s by Ewing Marion Kauffman with a mission statement to "foster a society of economically independent individuals who are engaged citizens in their communities." Their focus on grant making and operations focuses on two key areas – education and entrepreneurship. The belief is that a quality education is the foundation for self-sufficiency, preparing young people for success in college, life and business. Educated young adults will work for entrepreneurs possibly becoming entrepreneurs themselves, which provides jobs and wealth for society. The foundation works nationwide to advance the entrepreneurial spirit in which job creation, innovation and thus the economy prosper.

In 2004, Carl Schramm, then president of the Kauffman Foundation, published a groundbreaking essay stating that Americans have "literally no conception of the secret that truly underlies our economic success, and that for the United States to survive and continue to lead the world's economy, it is imperative we learn to understand and employ that secret." So, what's the secret? Our unparalleled skill as entrepreneurs! Entrepreneurs are what make the United States an economic superpower. Other countries have surpassed the United States in both technology and education. It is the unbridled economic will that still continues to set this country apart.

Intertwined with the work of the Kauffman Foundation, the Roosevelt Institute echoes the same pro-entrepreneurial spirit. Their project, the Next American Economy, identifies the trends and challenges that will shape our economy in the next 25 years to better inform the policy decisions we must make today. Bo Cutter is a Senior Fellow and Director of the Next American Economy Project. He works with a committee of experts to further new demands from the entrepreneurial community that plays such a vital role in this country's economic engine. In 2014, the Next American Economy has moved from the discussion stage into reality and plans to focus intently on new entrepreneurial platforms as a major contributor to economic growth over the next 25 years.

Teaching entrepreneurship to children is becoming much more prolific. In our household, both my husband and I proudly wear the badge of entrepreneur, no matter what the economy looks like, and teach our children the concepts of creating their own opportunity. Organizations like Disney are getting in on the game of entrepreneurship too. Hot Shot Business is an Internet game developed by the Kauffman Foundation where kids have the chance to run a business in Opportunity City on Disney.com.

The Enlightened Corporation

I sit with entrepreneurs every day and hear their dreams of grossing $5 million, $10 million, and even $50 million. These are all companies starting in garages, much like Google, Microsoft, Ford, etc. What will make them different when they meet their goals? What will prevent them from becoming the next corporate terrorists? If your company grows to the level of revenues you project, what will prevent you from doing just that? Will you do everything in your power to avoid causing harm to the next generation of small businesses hoping to meet their goals just like you?

As a company grows, you are faced with new challenges and opportunities. Meeting with huge success can make it difficult to remember those humble beginnings. You don't want to be the playground bully and resort to his terrorist antics. You don't aspire to be the recipient of a controversial, highly publicized government bailout. You want your company to grow in a productive, efficient way that contributes to you, your family, your team, your customers and the economy as a whole. Staying true to your vision while you travel your personal path on the trajectory from Garage to Great.

Sometimes the biggest help we can receive toward meeting our goals is not to learn additional things but to instead be reminded of what we already know. Consistency can be an entrepreneurs Achilles heel. It is easy to fall prey to spending your days putting out fires and to not use resources to proceduralize your operation. It's a catastrophic catch-22. You feel that if you turn your back on the client to spend time developing the procedure, the client will suffer from your turned back. So, you turn your back on the procedure to focus on mitigating the immediate client issue. And your company doesn't move forward. Break out of this trend with the principles we've covered here.

Get Cozy with Your Vision

There is a strange phenomenon that happens with a very aggressive vision. You believe it. You can share it with friends or professional colleagues that share your enthusiasm for the upside of small business, but what about when you are sharing that vision with black and white, nuts and bolts experts? Are you as comfortable sharing your vision with your accountant as you are with your childhood best friend? As comfortable sharing with your bank's underwriter as you are your mother? If not, get more comfortable with your vision. The way to get more comfortable with your vision is to have a well thought out, detailed plan of how you will get from where you are to where your vision sees you.

It is critically important to the success of your vision that you are just as comfortable sharing your vision in the boardroom as you are in a wine bar. If you have done your homework, this should be the case.

Crazy goals are only crazy if you haven't worked out exactly how you're going to get there. Every entrepreneur with a big goal has been met with raised eyebrows. The pioneers take the arrows. How are you going to get past that and get to your goals?

In *Think and Grow Rich*, Napoleon Hill was famous for saying, "Your achievement can be no greater than your plans are sound." What is your ultimate goal for achievement? Do you have a plan and know exactly what it looks like? "I want to gross $50 million" is not a plan. It's a vision. Take that $50 million and break it down into manageable action steps that you can take to accomplish your goal.

Scaling vs Growing – What's the Difference?

Entrepreneurs want their companies to grow. But often what is missing from the way in which they ask the question of "why" is their understanding of the difference between growing and scaling. I distinguish between growing and scaling because they are two very different things. Think of a tsunami and a hydroelectric plant. Both have a ton of water but they handle that water in completely different ways.

A tsunami is uncontrolled water. It is like growth. Growth happens. Often, it happens whether you have a proactive plan for it or not. Unconscious growth creates a situation in which once the upper limit of what the entrepreneur can handle is met, the problems start and the entrepreneur just can't juggle any more balls. So, the company falters.

Scaling is like a hydroelectric plant. It still handles a ton of water. But in a controlled state, it creates electricity. Scaling is an articulate, conscious growth that is well thought out and planned for. You, as the entrepreneur, anticipate the growth. You put in place innovation, organization, systems, customer service parameters – in short, you put in place the principles of The Entrepreneurial Standard to ensure that the growth you experience in your company is scalable and not a tsunami that stops you in your tracks.

Channel your focus on scaling so you can create electricity and conscious growth in your business.

Putting These Principles to Work

The Entrepreneurial Standard is about breaking through the small business ceiling to grow strategically and profitably.

As an entrepreneur you no doubt have aggressive goals for yourself and for your company. You know where "there" is. So how are you going to get there? Eight out of ten small businesses fail. Out of those that succeed, a large percentage don't outlive their original founder. A large percentage also get stuck at a ceiling of what they can aspire to. Have you hit that ceiling? You know when it happens...you grow to a certain size and then it seems like everything begins to go wrong. That for every step you take forward you take one step back. For every new client you gain you lose one, putting you back at the same level.

How do you ensure that each client receives a consistent product, or has the same customer service experience? How do you focus on working on your company and not in it 100% of the time? How do you stay consistently focused on making the big decisions? Balancing innovation with organization? You stay focused with a laser precision on the things that will get you there. This book has covered some of them, but there are more. You truly can become the company you envision in your biggest dreams. But it doesn't happen by accident. And it doesn't happen unconsciously. You take an active role in the practices, systems and mantras that make it so.

We've seen that what scares and excites you changes as your company grows. When you first start your company, the level of decision making you must embark on is small relative to that which you must face once your company is big and while your company is scaling. But each of those decisions is a critical building block to your company's success. Some of the principles we've covered here may seem overwhelming or a bit scary. There are, after all, bigger fish to fry in a bigger company. Take it one step at a time. You will find that as you move forward the footfalls will come faster and faster. You may take a little longer to reach your goal for what Great means to your company, or you may be an overnight sensation that is thrown into full implementation of all of these concepts in the blink of an eye. At the same time, as the company grows you will by default become more and more removed from the details and the day to day.

Once when cashflow was tight in my company, I had a longer conversation with my office manager regarding a $100 office supply order than a client of mine did with their CFO about a $2 million property purchase. Who do you think met their goals for their company more quickly? The fires present themselves. Entrepreneurs are held to the highest standards of knowing everything and doing everything. But at the same time, they must create everything. Follow trailblazers before you that have already created the wheel. Bring in as many resources as you can afford. It will promote your growth, increase your bandwidth and allow you to focus on the big picture of your company. In my company, I had to learn to step away from the smaller conversations in order for my company to grow and for me to meet my goals.

Some Thoughts Before You Go

Believing in the power of entrepreneurship is the first step to realizing this massive economic force and scaling your company to the next level. Don Shula said, "It's the start that stops most people." Whether it is doubt in one's ability or a sense of feeling overwhelmed of all of the steps of opening your doors, becoming an entrepreneur can seem a daunting prospect.

Even more daunting can be breaking through any limitations to your growth and taking your business to the next level. One million is a magical number. This is the goal for countless entrepreneurs. And the truth is...the first million is the hardest. Once your company is grossing seven figures you have been forced to put in place certain things. Utilize the practices in this book to take those systems and make them run with minimal involvement from you as CEO. It will enable you to conquer the next one, two, three or ten million more easily. You are only one person – and this counts in both your personal and professional life. Throwing more of your time at your company in a desperate attempt to increase your capacity to grow your company is not the answer. It's not working harder. It's working smarter. That is what The Entrepreneurial Standard is all about. At its very core it's about increasing your bandwidth, crystallizing your focus and maximizing your effectiveness.

Here are some guidelines to making sure you start strong and keep growing:

1. *Naysayers Be Gone.* Don't seek advice of too many people who view risk as unnecessary. There will be plenty of people that think you've gone nuts when you tell them about your venture or

your goal for its ultimate success. It can be family, life-long friends, your spouse or nosy passersby. Don't let this be a detractor if you feel the passion to pursue the venture.

2. *Do Your Homework.* But don't go running out the door without doing your homework. The best way to prove those naysayers right is to pull the trigger prematurely without doing some very thorough homework. You need to know what your products are, who your customers are, what your costs are, and much more before you spring your new company on the world.

3. *Create Your Own Luck.* Strong, profitable, longstanding businesses don't just happen. They are born of hard work, tenacity, street smarts, grit and passion for your product. You create your own good luck by possessing these traits.

4. *Know What You Don't Know.* You don't know everything. No one does. Don't try to know everything. Support yourself with experts that will help you get the ball into the end zone. Not only will they have more depth of knowledge than you can get by Googling their expertise to try to save a buck, but they will save you time by not having to recreate the wheel to get off the ground.

5. *Hail Pareto and Drucker!* Pareto's principle says that 80% of your results come from 20% of your efforts. Peter Drucker said, "What gets measured

gets managed." Measure what is getting you your results. Chances are it's coming from 20% of your efforts. Constant measurement of these two concepts in connection with each other will keep you profitable, efficient and sane.

6. *Failure Improves Success.* If you could have a do-over on your adversities, would you? How many times have you looked back at the mistakes, tribulations and stressors that got you to where you are and said, "God, if I only knew then what I know now, I would have handled that so differently, protected myself, fought harder," and so on. But it's really a fake sense of knowledge. You are who you are because of those adversities. Use them to your advantage and learn from them going forward.

There is a premise in business that success is a straight-line trajectory. This is not the case. The road to riches as an entrepreneur can be paved with many ups and downs. Entrepreneurship can often be a successful venture only after you have experienced failure. This is how you learn and build a better business. If you are starting over (at any age) focus on the key concepts of becoming an entrepreneur and not "what should have been" or a preset time line that you have now missed by having to start over in a new venture. Focusing on what will be rather than what might have been will allow you to meet with success that much faster.

A First Class State of Mind

I recently flew to Toronto on a business trip and had upgraded to first class. When you are able to reward yourself with this, you arrive with a completely different demeanor. Everyone knows the back of the plane is horrible. The seats are smaller, they seldom recline, the flight crew is usually out of snacks and you're right next to the bathroom. First class comes complete with china, hot towels and warm cookies. Blankets when it's cold and wine being refilled in flight. It's a completely different universe a mere six feet from coach.

Regardless of what your idea of first class is – whether it is flying first class or being able to take mini "retirements" with your family – being an entrepreneur allows you to create your own economy and create your own wealth – you decide whether you ride in the front of the metaphorical plane or the back. You can focus not on how much the upgrade to first class costs, but instead focus on "what do I need to create in order for the cost of this to be completely affordable to me?"

How can you scale your company to give you what you want and be the company of your dreams? The goal here is to rule your world. Create your own luck. Make your own economy. You too will take your company to the heights you see in your future just like those trailblazing entrepreneurs before you. Wherever your "there" is, make it yours, make it real and make it there with The Entrepreneurial Standard.

ABOUT THE AUTHOR

Tanya McCaffery is passionate about entrepreneurship. Through her unique approach to accounting, she works to empower small business CEOs with financial information that allows them to meet the benchmarks they have set for their company and for themselves. Tanya is the President and CEO of VAST Powered by The CFO Group and works with countless entrepreneurs in helping them take their companies from where they "are" to where they "want". To help with that mission, Tanya's extensive accounting and finance team at VAST Headquarters in the beautiful Reno/Tahoe area provides a full range of virtual accounting, tax and CFO services to hundreds of small businesses throughout the US and in seven countries. VAST brings the horsepower of a Fortune 500 level accounting department to the small business. It truly is better for your bottom line.

To learn more about how VAST can help take your company to the next level, visit us at any of our sites:
www.vastcfo.com
www.thecfogroup.com
www.facebook.com/CFO.TanyaMcCaffery

Be sure to opt in to VAST: Track, our educational series for entrepreneurs, to receive even more helpful information on growing and scaling your business.

VAST Powered by The CFO Group, Inc.
4745 Caughlin Parkway, Suite 200
Reno, NV 89519
(775)359-7600

Made in the USA
San Bernardino, CA
05 January 2017